The Norman Manley Memorial Lectures 1984 - 1995

HANSIB CARIBBEAN

in association with
THE NORMAN MANLEY MEMORIAL LECTURE COMMITTEE

First published in 1996 by Hansib Publishing (Caribbean) Ltd
PO Box 2773, St John's, Antigua, WI
in association with
The Norman Manley Memorial Lecture Committee
28 Hillbury Avenue, Kenton, Harrow HA3 8EW

Distributed in the United Kingdom by Readers Book Club
Third Floor, Tower House, 141-149 Fonthill Road, London N4 3HF
Fax: 0171-263 9656

Printed in the United Kingdom by Martins the Printers Ltd
Berwick Upon Tweed

British Library Cataloguing in Publication Data.
A catalogue record for this book is available from the British Library

ISBN 976-8163-00-3

NORMAN MANLEY COMMITTEE MEMBERS

Contents

Acknowledgements

This book would not be possible without the support and generosity of

Professor Stuart Hall
The Hon Vivian Blake
Sir Shridath Ramphal
The Rt Hon Michael Manley
Mr Bill Morris
The Rt Hon Tony Benn

Jamaica Producers PLC
Tate and Lyle PLC
Cable and Wireless PLC
Transport and General Workers Union
Hansib Caribbean
The Jamaica High Commission

The encouragement given to the Lecture Committee of volunteers has enabled this publication to be available to the wider public and included with this are our thanks to all those who have supported the Lectures either by attending or by their donations.

Publisher's note

Readers unfamiliar with Hansib's publications may note the use of 'Westindies' (not 'West Indies'). This has been used in all Hansib publications since 1973 in a tribute to the formation of the Caribbean Community (CariCom) at Chaguaramas, Trinidad, on 4 July 1973 and as an appropriation of the name given by the "discoverers" to assert the region's united, unique and distinctive identity.

The Norman Manley Memorial Lecture Committee

I n 1983, on the occasion when Jamaica celebrated its 21st year of Independence from British colonial rule, Jamaica's then High Commissioner to the United Kingdom, Mr H S Walker, felt there should be special projects to mark the event. Having assembled a group of advisers to bounce ideas around, one suggestion was advanced that a series of events depicting the nation's heritage should be highlighted.

Norman Manley, being the architect of modern Jamaica and one of its national heroes, was identified as one individual on whom emphasis should be focused. It was then suggested that as a tribute to him, Memorial Lectures should be organised.

The idea was accepted and a Memorial Lecture Committee, initially headed by the High Commissioner was formed. The first lecture was planned under the chairmanship of Miss Linda Haye and delivered by Professor Stuart Hall, at the Royal Commonwealth Society in July 1984. The second, again under her chairmanship was delivered by the Hon Vivian Blake QC OJ, at the same venue in July 1986. The third, under the chairmanship of Leslie Scafe was delivered by Sir Shridath Ramphal in June 1988 at the Royal Commonwealth Society. Under the chairmanship of Roy Henry, the fourth was delivered by the Rt Hon Michael Manley, at the London School of Economics in October 1992. The fifth, under acting chairman Lensworth Small was delivered by Mr Bill Morris, at Transport House in December 1993; and the sixth under the chairmanship of Mrs Icelyn Gray JP, was delivered by the Rt Hon Tony Benn MP, at the Commonwealth Institute in July 1995.

All these lectures are aimed at instilling in us the ideals that made Norman Manley such an influence on life, not only in Jamaica and the Caribbean, but the world at large, in the belief that we may draw inspiration from this great man and strive to achieve excellence in our endeavours.

Foreword

Because it is so lucid and clear this book needs little introduction except for the purpose of emphasising its current relevance. One of the prices that immigrants have to pay when they tend to drift away from their cultural roots and lose out on the stimulation and motivation of the life and works of outstanding people in their society of origin. The lives of those people are exemplars and role models for the emulation of succeeding generations. There are some people who view this rupture as no bad thing and certainly preferable to the confusion and indecision of those who attempt to live in two cultures.

There is, however, the frightening danger that in the absence of information of their cultural roots succeeding generations will slide into a social malaise and alienation if they feel that their adopted society is treating them as non-persons without significant historical roots.

These were the considerations in our minds when a group of us in 1983 gladly responded to an invitation to become members of the Norman Manley Memorial Committee. The main function of the committee is to arrange lectures in memory of the outstanding contribution made by one of the founding fathers of the Jamaican nation. We felt that it was necessary both for ourselves, and to inform our children, grandchildren and great grandchildren and the wider society, of the moral and social values delineated in the life of this outstanding man.

We feel it is time that the first six Memorial Lectures reach the public bookshelves. The first was delivered by Professor Stuart Hall, who like Norman Manley was a Rhodes Scholar. His lecture **"Through the Passage of Time"** gave clear direction to the Lecture Committee particularly the chapter which states: "It was Manley's outstanding contribution to have upheld the best of that class to the people, to have insisted that they turn their face towards the progressive line, in facing the problems of autonomy and independence. He gave leadership to his class, and through his class, to the people, and for that reason to the nation.

His career does not require us to overcome or shirk the problems he confronted, the deep legacy and tensions of colonial dependency which remain to ravage our people.

He was not a superman, but he was, for all that, a man of his time and a Leader and Founder of the Nation."

In the second lecture **"The Pursuit of Excellence"** given by the

Hon. Vivian Blake, OJ, QC, former Chief Justice of the Bahamas and former law pupil and colleague in law and politics of the late Right Excellent Norman Manley, he made reference to a passage from a speech made by Norman Manley to the members of the Philadelphia Bar Association in 1967, when he discusses Jamaica's aims in relation to the attainment of racial harmony, and defines the fundamental prerequisite of true racial integration with eloquent simplicity: and he said: "We do not seek mere tolerance between people of different races and admixtures. What we aim at is a society in which the races of mankind live together in mutual harmony and respect and affection: where the value of a person has nothing at all to do with his race or the colour of his skin. In a word we press on to the end where colour has ceased to have any psychological significance in society.

Let me make it clear - a society which still talks about racial tolerance has not yet reached or is barely at the first stage of the process of racial integration. No society will achieve the true goal until colour ceases to have psychological importance in the mind of the society itself. It may take a thousand years, but the world will not be civilised until that goal is finally achieved."

The first two lectures in this series commemorate the life and work of Norman Washington Manley and are concerned with Manley and Jamaica. The third Memorial Lecture **"No Island is an Island"** given by Sir Shridath S. Ramphal, then Commonwealth Secretary General cast the net of analysis and reminiscence somewhat wider and covered the theme of the Caribbean otherwise known as the West Indies. It is a theme that was central to Norman Manley's life and work.

"Today, as we look to the 21st Century, the truth every part of the West Indies must respect and to which each West Indian must respond is that 'No Island is an Island Entire of Itself'. Every inch of our West Indian region from Belize to Guyana is a piece of one nation a part of one people, a bit of one world. The vision of West Indian Nationhood that Norman Manley cherished has only sharpened with the passing years. Its pursuit will remain our central challenge until eventually we reach it."

It seemed fitting that the fourth Lecture **"Caribbean Co-operation - The Imperative For Survival"** was delivered by the Rt Hon. Michael Manley, former Prime Minister of Jamaica, inspired by the vision of his late father who in his lecture said the over-riding cause of his sense of intimidation, reflected on a speech his father made in Kingston in 1947 at a meeting of a body called the Caribbean Labour Congress, and I quote:

7

"I say it is not hard to see what we are to do. The history of all nations is a history of amalgamation from small things to large. I say it is evident that we must create out of ourselves a large enough unit to do two things. First to satisfy the growing ambition of our people for an area of action large enough for their creative energies; and the West Indies is full of creative energy, as full as any place in the world today. I say we must create a large enough area, small though it may be in the face of the colossal who bestride the world today, but a large enough area to give us a voice and pull and power over those international affairs which in the long run determine the peace and prosperity and the opportunity for happiness of the three million people of these lands.

"I say, the second ambition must be to take what we have together to plan it for a national future for our people. Let any man examine his conscience and speak for his own country and ask himself 'Do I feel capable?' And if we dare speak the truth and this is an occasion when truth should be spoken we are bound to admit that the very fact of size and the very fact of limitations imposed by that size makes the task almost insuperable."

Two very interesting questions emerged from Michael Manley's lecture is whether N W Manley's vision as he expressed it in 1947 is relevant today? And why did the attempt at Federation fail?

Bill Morris, General Secretary of the Transport and General Workers' Union who gave the fifth lecture **"Rich World, Poor World: Squaring The Circle"** focused on some of N W Manley's ideals as a socialist with a broader internationalist vision who believed that collective effort and involvement was absolutely necessary to turn personal values and beliefs into realities. "Through history and across the world, two forces have always been present in the liberation struggle. Wherever there is oppression, wherever there is discrimination, wherever there is disadvantage and inequality - organised labour and the churches have always worked for freedom. And Manley identifies with both."

Bill thinks "that Norman Manley would have approved of the global approach. His experience in the liberation struggle led him to understand that, in the modern world, independence was a means to freedom, not an end in itself. He believed that success could only come from recognising that nations are interdependent, and that they must work together for the common benefit of their peoples. The nations of the Caribbean have come to accept a great deal of Manley's vision. He hoped that the wider world community will one day do the same. Only then can we guarantee that 'the people shall govern'."

When we met with Tony Benn at his residence to discuss the sixth Memorial Lecture, we decided that the title should be **"A Vision Of**

The Future" there was some scepticism as to the slant on which his lecture would focus. But when reading his lecture it is clear, and he said it, that he was thinking aloud about those things that would have concerned Norman Manley in his time and will concern future generations. What he was really saying is that what Norman Manley fought for, the ballot box, would give you some control over your destiny, but it is now being taken away again in the guise of competitive productivity.

Tony Benn, in summing up, said "I believe Norman Manley inspired a nation to so believe it had done it itself, and that is why it is worth commemorating his memory and continue with these lectures so that none of us forget the quality of the leadership that he gave to his people and to the human race."

All the lectures in one way or another describe Norman Manley as an absolutely mythical character - a great scholar, a lawyer, a distinguished parliamentarian, a soldier, a world statesman, founder of the People's National Party an athlete, a teacher, a founder of the nation and national hero - someone who really contributed immensely to the development of Jamaica and to its place in the world. He was a great citizen of a small nation.

The greatness of Manley lay in the very choice he made; not only to turn from being a recognised and pre-eminent barrister to the uncertain destiny of politics, not only to choose to be a citizen of a small nation, but above all to help create that nation as an independent entity. There are many memorials to what Manley did for Jamaica and to how he expressed himself through being a Jamaican, but the truest memorial to Manley was, as is to be expected, spoken by Manley himself in 1961 after the drafting of the Independence Constitution for Jamaica, he said then.

"We have just completed a great work, the draft of a Constitution for an Independent Jamaica. Twenty-three years ago I challenged history by demanding self-government for Jamaica and by dedicating my life to its achievement. Now independence has come and history challenges us.' He achieved what he set out to achieve.

I commend these lectures for use in the social and cultural sections of our educational development programme.

Icelyn A. Gray J.P.
Chairman
September, 1996

9

The First Norman Manley Memorial Lecture

Delivered at the Royal Commonwealth Society Hall, Northumberland Avenue, London, on 6 July 1984 by Professor Stuart Hall. The Chairman of the proceedings was His Excellency Mr H S Walker, CD, High Commissioner of Jamaica.

"Through the Passage of Time"

It is difficult for me to express the honour which I feel to have been invited to deliver the Norman Manley Memorial Lecture this evening. There are certainly many in the room whose faces I recognise already who knew Norman Manley better than I did, who shared his life and his work, his causes and activities, and his hopes and ambitions for the country. I hope that at least some of the things I say will strike a chord of memory and that at least some of the judgements I offer will win your assent and accord. I want to say something first of all about his life because we are speaking of someone whose life and political career are deeply and closely and intimately intertwined.

Manley's father was the illegitimate son of a woman of the people. His grandfather was a Yorkshire man. In the classic pattern of the times, he married the post mistress at Porus, a woman almost white, half sister of Bustamante's father. Her mother had married twice.

Norman Manley was born in 1893 in Roxborough, Manchester, a small property near Porus. His father died while he was still young, leaving relatively little. The family was not well off. His mother emigrated for a time to the United States in order to keep the family together. It is certainly his mother's determination, survival capacity and above all her pledge to foster the education of her children which made the early imprint on Manley's life. She was a woman of considerable independence; she was both overseer and manager of the small estate at Belmont, St Catherine where Norman grew up. The place, incidentally, from which Alexander Bustamante emigrated as a young man of 21 to Cuba. They were of course cousins.

In his early schooling, Manley went first of all to Wolmers until the money ran out, and then to elementary school, and then to Beckfords and Smiths in Spanish Town, and finally in 1906 on a scholarship to Jamaica College. He said of himself:

"I grew up a Bushman... I earned my pocket money clearing pastures and chipping log wood at standard rates. I would go out in the morning and share lunch with the workers and if we were out looking for stray cattle, would walk all day and get home late at night after 12 to 14 hours on the constant move."

He came, in short, from the struggling, respectable country middle class, not the well educated, well endowed, fast lane, city middle class. He came from the backbone of creole Jamaica. He said he never went to a party in Jamaica until he returned there in 1923. Reflecting later on those who accused him of being irretrievably middle class, too Oxford-trained and too endowed and imbued with the legal temper, Norman Manley remarked:

"They don't know that I grew up with working people in deep rural Jamaica, and even in England and France before I went to Oxford, I spent four years as a private in the army where my own sergeant was a Covent Garden market porter and half the men were either Yorkshire miners or East End workers."

His principal schooling was at Jamaica College. He found it, as I did, a tough school. He was part of a rather rebellious group of boys. At 14 he resolved to turn over a new leaf. He went to the Headmaster, R M Murray, a name familiar I am sure to many of you, and set about persuading Mr Murray that he was going to become a serious scholar and go for the Rhodes. First of all he cut himself adrift from the rebellious group of young people, then he turned seriously to his studies and then seriously to athletics where he shone. The death of his mother in this period moved him considerably but didn't halt his career. Part of his family went with his eldest sister to England, but Manley settled with friends to continue to study and to excel on the playing field. When he left Jamaica College he taught briefly at Barnes School, at Jamaica College itself. He won the Rhodes at Titchfield in 1914.

Shortly before he left Jamaica for England, he had a long illness, typhoid fever, quite a common occurrence at that time. It had a profound personal effect upon him: he said afterwards that it had transformed him from 'the hardest and most ruthless of young men into a man capable of discovering a new range of emotional understanding.' It was one of many turning points.

You will forgive me a brief digression on the Rhodes scholarship. I was fortunate enough to be a Rhodes scholar in 1950, as your Chairman has said, those of us who are Rhodes scholars have a deeply ambivalent relationship to it. We are considerably grateful for the opportunities which it provided us to go abroad to complete our education. On the other hand it is not possible to forget that Cecil Rhodes was one of the great adventurer scoundrels of the imperialist period and his career wrought havoc in Central, East and South Africa. It is not on record what Norman Manley though of the Rhodes scholarship. I am grateful to say he had the acumen to sit on my Rhodes Board and give me one (laughter). I am grateful to say that I had the acumen not to refuse it, but I want nevertheless to make clear the terms on which young men in those days had to find education. Manley had what was coming to him - one of the few scholarships available which enabled one to go abroad to study. He was by then an illustrious scholar, a thriving and pushing young man, an outstanding athlete and, of course, he seized his chance. We have some sense of what kind of person he was already at that stage: by nature still, instinctively, a rebel, with a passionate interest in ideas, reading everything that came to hand. He himself said that he was 'of a deeply sceptical outlook.' It's a feature which never left him. Above all, he loved talk and argument. Why else would he have become a lawyer? Indeed, it wasn't at all certain what he would read at Oxford, his family, knowing that he couldn't leave an argument alone, said: 'He had better read law.'

It was shortly after coming to England for the first time that he met his wife-to-be, his cousin, a young lady at that stage only 14 years old, 'strange, shy, highly individualist,' whom he married in 1921. He went to Jesus College, Oxford, to study law, but his legal and academic career was interrupted by the war. He decided not, as was open to him, to enlist as an officer, but to enlist in the ordinary rank and file as a soldier, and by choice he spent three years on the Western Front. He was present at the Battle of the Somme at Ypres where he lost an elder brother. He was decorated with the Military Medal for bravery in action. He returned to complete his career at Oxford and won first class honours in the Bar Finals. He was the leading Prizeman at Gray's Inn. He was called to the Bar in 1921 and studied briefly in Chambers in England before returning to Jamaica in 1922 with, as he said himself, 'a wife, a baby, a profession and clear sum of £50.'

There began his formidable and illustrious career at the Bar. A career at the Bar in Jamaica is no ordinary thing, for it was one of the few professions at that time open to the independent middle class. It was a position of considerable social, and later of considerable political, authority. To be an active member of the Bar was a matter of distinction. To be, as Norman Manley became, the leading advocate at the Jamaican

Bar, with extraordinary gifts of legal brilliance and forensic eloquence, was an outstanding achievement.

He remarked about the condition of Jamaica on his return, that he was shocked that so few, if any, Jamaicans were interested in anything except the daily round of events. He said the economy was turgid and there was a general air of emptiness, but 'for a time I did not study it, I merely met it. It rolled over me leaving me feeling almost in despair.' Instead he set about establishing an independent life with his wife and young family at Drumblair where he lived for 38 years until 1962. It was a happy and supportive family life with a wife who made an outstanding and independent contribution of her own to the cultural life of the nation. He was, however, not long out of the political limelight. He became involved in the establishment of the Jamaica Banana Producers Association, a cooperative intended in part to defend the position of the independent small farmers against the massive control exerted at the time by the big companies involved in the banana and sugar trade. In the course of this first historic cooperative venture, he said: 'I learned overnight an enormous amount about the social and economic conditions of Jamaica and about the industry.' He came back from those negotiations with an important benefit for the people: one cent US per bunch of bananas, for the general good and welfare of the ordinary people of Jamaica as the foundation of the Jamaica Welfare Limited. He was chairman for ten years, and its impact on the social life of Jamaica has not been fully estimated or acknowledged.

We are at 1938. It is a historic turning-point in the advance of the people towards independence. It begins with the consequences of a world economic depression, biting deep and hard on the people of the Caribbean, and on the unrest which swept the country and accompanied the birth of the Jamaican labour movement. Manley acknowledged the need for a political party in Jamaica 'dedicated to the cause of the ordinary working people.' It was a time of ferment, the rousing of a challenge to the old crown colony government; also the moment of the birth and formation of the Peoples National Party.

This party brought a range of progressive and nationalist-oriented organisations and individuals into a great national progressive movement for independence and autonomy in the Caribbean. Under the leadership of what I want to call the national progressive wing of the middle class, numbers of people of all kinds, from different quarters and parts of Jamaican society, began to glimpse for the first time the possibility of independence. It was a movement which Norman Manley as the young legal intellectual shared with his cousin, Bustamante, at that point in time the undisputed leader of the trades union movement. Those Jamaicans whose memories are long enough will recall that the

Bustamante Industrial Trade Union was indeed the labour wing of the PNP. Bustamante himself took a prominent part in the Ward Theatre meeting at which the Peoples National Party was launched.

Between the historic events of 1938 and the constitution and election of 1944, is the birth of modern Jamaican politics. Whatever is right and, indeed, whatever is wrong about Jamaican politics, had something to do with that period. It is a formative period. It is the historical moment when the thing first takes shape, when the parameters are established, it is when we enter a new kind of history.

There is hardly any point asking whether we went into it right ways on. History actually wasn't asking us whether we wanted to go into it at all. We went into it and it had a certain shape, and these are the men who shaped it. Our duty today is to understand the historical process by which they were formed, to understand the strength and the limits of the political system they established and the inspirations they offered to move it forward.

This is the birth of Jamaican politics and the processes which have moulded it ever since. The intent above all to hold, to constrain, the enormous tensions of a still colonial society, the enormous contradictory pressures of a dependent colonial economy within the framework of parliamentary democracy. It is one of the most audacious political attempts ever tried in the history of decolonisation.

It is a remarkable irony that, having laid the base and struggled for and demanded adult suffrage, Manley and the PNP lost the 1944 election, indeed that he was not to be in power until 1955.

I want to say a word now about the basic political structure which emerged at this time. On the one hand, the Jamaica Labour Party, with its base in the rural and urban dispossessed, brought about a coalition between the massed ranks of the dispossessed and elements in the leading section of the commercial classes. A formidable popular block, it presented one kind of political choice to the Jamaican people, a choice on the whole committed to the free enterprise system at home and to the open door system abroad. The other choice was the coalition of the progressive middle classes, the urban and rural middle class, farming elements and those sections of organised labour which were organised under the TUC rather than under the Bustamante Industrial Trade Union, which drifted into the orbit of social democracy and that particular form of constitutionalist nationalism for which Manley and the PNP came to stand.

One of the most remarkable facts of the Jamaican political system is the stability with which that double choice has endowed it. It stands of course in the historical narrative and asks something about the nature of the politics of this figure, Norman Manley, who had arisen to dominate in part the political stage.

First of all I refer to his commitment to organised politics itself as a precondition of nationhood. He had a firm belief in what I can only call the civilising process of politics itself. He believed that the ordinary people of the country should have the opportunity to exercise political choice and become involved in a politics which mattered, with the power to do something dangling at the end of it; and that the only route to that was the increasing organisation of the people within the framework of political movements. He said no amount of benevolent administration, no amount of contribution towards making a happy and contented people, will ever produce a nation unless you have a political organisation that shares and marches with the destiny of the nation as a whole. He wrote: 'I am a Jamaican who takes the view that politics is essential to a civilised nation and to the development of nationality to every order in the world.' In the early stages the Peoples National Party was more a movement than a party in the normal sense, more like a Congress Party than like the Labour Party. It is only with the spirit of 1942 and the emergence of the two party system that the PNP becomes a fully organised political party in the Western liberal democratic sense of the term. Manley's commitment to that evolution was unswerving.

Secondly, I want to note that his project at that stage of his political career was to uphold national alliance, embracing people of all kinds and of all sections and of all classes, particularly those willing to come together under two major political programmes: universal adult suffrage and the advance through self-government to nationhood.

The ability to commit himself to the democratic process of a universalistic kind, gradually to move away from the limited franchise on which the majority of people in Jamaica had to exercise their political choice, was a commitment of the first order in his political career. The driving force of his political life at this stage, and in a sense throughout his political career, was the drive of self-government and nationhood. He believed in the transfer of power from the limited colonial constitution to a fully elected, fully democratic nation, the basis for the emergence of modern mass politics in Jamaica.

There were other commitments that are of crucial importance in defining the political character of the man. One was the commitment to labour. Manley believed that the attempt to raise the standard of living of the common people could not happen without the labour movement. Any man who pretends to be progressive and who procures his ends by attempting to subvert the course of this movement is no friend of his country. Of course, as an Oxford-trained barrister, he had a distance to make up between himself and that of the leaders of the urban and rural masses.

Besides, his orientation was never labourist in a narrow sense. It was overridingly nationalist. That is to say, constantly he would go back to the cross-class appeal for self-government, rather than to the narrow, more sectional appeal of a labourist politician. He saw the critical importance of trade union organisation, which has in different ways been in crucial alliance with the PNP throughout its political history. He saw it as a bridge between the middle class movement for self-government on the one hand and the working class movement which implied social and economic reconstruction on the other. The political organisation which brought together these two wings of politics constituted his particular and distinguished political vision.

Manley was of course also a socialist. He advised on the constitution of the Peoples National Party, which in 1940 formally declared itself a socialist organisation. What did that mean? 'It was not,' he said, 'a commitment either to revolution or to Godlessness.' He acknowledged quite often what he called 'the mixed ancestry of ideas' which had gone into the formation of his own socialism. He is indebted to both liberal and socialist thought. This is a matter of interpretation and I offer it as such.

In my view, his socialism was essentially a commitment to social and economic justice, to the idea of the rational planning of administration and economic life, to the notions of reform and cooperation and to public ownership insofar as it was required for the transformation of a dependent economy into that of an independent and autonomous one. 'It is not true,' he said, 'that all socialist thought involves the overthrow of the State by revolution.' Indeed, in another place he said: 'The essence of British socialism, democratic socialism, to which I subscribe, is equality.' In my view there is no question that this was his national and political formation. There is a remarkable consistency, inspite of all the situations and pressures that he faced throughout his political life to return to those bearings in a highly distinctive tradition of liberal social democracy. And if you want to get a bearing on a man who, in not very propitious circumstances, sought to declare his commitment to socialism, I think you have to understand that in the context of another feature, that is to say, his constitutionalism.

Manley was also a constitutionalist socialist. For one thing, he had the enormous privilege of actually helping to draft a constitution, but he was also a lawyer, and a lawyer brought up in the English tradition is a constitutionalist by instinct and intuition. He knew as well how to make as how to break constitutions. But above the question of making a new constitution for the nation was his commitment to the constitutional tradition of a parliamentary framework. During the 1944 election, when Manley accepted the role of Opposition Leader within the highly restricted 1944 Constitution rather than in the open and

16

independent constitution that many people hoped for, he expressed himself as dissatisfied with the pace of advance but willing to work within the terms the constitution offered him for the sake of unity. When I say that it is not an empty phrase because he had in front of him the duty to construct - across the division between the political parties and the different social groups within the society - a consensus around the drive to independence. For the sake of unity, he said he would work (within the limited powers which only reserved a number of areas of government in justice, defence and foreign policy) towards self-government in stages.

In 1955 when finally the party was elected to power he was in charge of the logistics of the peaceful transfer of power, and he operated to move the country through those stages into independence in partnership less than in struggle with the other person at that stage in charge of the Jamaican social formation, Sir Hugh Foot (later Lord Caradon).

Manley's commitment to constitutionalism was not only formal: he was a constitutionalist to the backbone. I recall that he refused to report to his own party conference in 1961 on the details of the independence constitution because he had not yet consulted with the opposition. He told the delegates: 'It is right that I should treat the opposition with the greatest respect and discuss no details until I have discussed the details with them.'

Nowhere is his constitutionalism clearer than in his commitment to the two party system. Not only because that is the political system which willy-nilly he and Bustamante framed. That is how it happened. The two charismatic figures, cousins but with opposing political commitments and opposing, sharply contrasting personalities, within them the two labour movements. That is to say a political system constructed around the two parties but penetrating deeply into the structure of the nation itself, a genuine, deep and lasting political division. It wasn't simply that that was the nature of the political system. It was the idea of that political system to which Manley was committed. He regarded it as providing the stability within which the nation could evolve. He recognised that the divisions were deep and would have to be so, but he said:

"The parties must not differ so widely in their ideas of government and society as to compel one to seek and eradicate totally or to destroy the other as an essential condition of the advancement of their aims."

Indeed, he regarded the two party system as both inevitable and right. Now the question of whether that has turned out to be the political framework within which the Jamaican people are most likely to find their historic destiny is a highly controversial one, and you would expect me to tread delicately around it. What I would say with respect to Manley and his times is whether you like it or not it was quite consistent. The man never thought anything else. Perhaps he ought to have thought, or he might have thought had he been different, born in a different place, grown up in a different culture, attuned to a different style, educated in a different way, surrounded by different friends, in a different era. Perhaps, but history is not made of perhapses, it is made of what happened and what happened is that was his commitment, that was his formation, that was his political outlook. He played a key role in bringing the parliamentary style of two party government into fruition in Jamaican political life.

It was not of course without its tensions. Forces to the left of him articulated a more radical politics, reflecting perhaps the deepening economic crisis, the growing poverty and unemployment of the period. There was the tragic split in the party which led, whatever you think of their politics, to the emigration and exodus from the labour movement of some of the most outstanding left intellectuals that Jamaica has ever produced: the tragic moment of the split in the party and the purge. The Cold War which fractured social democratic and socialist movements in the West everywhere, fractured and bit deeply into the PNP itself. It split asunder the Jamaican political movement, and in some ways that movement remains permanently scarred by its consequences.

So one mustn't imagine that Manley in this period, out of office in opposition, riding what is undoubtedly one of the most difficult and contradictory phases of the evolution of the nation, had an easy time. Nevertheless, when 1955 came and finally he acceded to power, he was at the height of his political stature and dominated the political scene. His electoral victories in 1955 and 1959 were outstanding. His particular strengths as a moulder of the nation and as a formidable parliamentary politician were at their height in this period. He was in command of the logistics of the nation.

He had a superb mastery of the House of Representatives. His parliamentary skills, his debating and oratorical gifts were turned to having the House at his command. It was not only an exercise in parliamentary government, it was a kind of continuous lesson from parliament to the people outside in the art of the transition to peaceful self-government. His major contribution in this period is as political administrator.

He improved terms of trade with foreign companies. He succeeded in setting terms which attracted substantial foreign capital investment in Jamaica. The tragedy was that this investment failed to keep step with unemployment, didn't achieve the equality in distribution which

18

he wanted and ultimately failed to break the leading strings of economic dependency.

The growth in the manufacturing and tourist sectors at this stage was impressive. His economic government was directed towards the aim of enabling the society to raise itself by its own efforts: Operation Bootstrap, as the Puerto Rican model was called. It is not a strap that has proved to be strong enough, but Manley certainly tested it out. He helped to democratise the education system. He expanded the system of primary schools, especially in the rural areas, and extended library facilities. As a man committed to ideas and to books he could not bear the thought that there wasn't a travelling library in most of the towns and rural enclaves of Jamaica.

He tried to bring about increasing support for rural agriculture and small farming. Through a gift of insight he took Jamaica into the Federation, but ironically it was the collapse of the referendum on that issue which precipitated his defeat in 1962. He framed the independence constitution of 1962, though, again with an irony which dogged his political career, when it came to be implemented he was already out of office.

Above all, in this period he brought a high-minded probity and sense of integrity to the high office of Chief Minister and then of Premier. His speech to the House in the independence constitution debate is a classic statement of liberal democratic constitutionalism. It is a speech of which Gladstone or Burke or Peel would have been proud. It seals Jamaica into place within the English constitutional tradition at the very moment that he is breaking from it. The continuities between past and future which are present in Manley's words at that time are more striking than the distance and the ruptures which he is making. It leads us to reflect once again on how complex are the connections between the Caribbean and the United Kingdom. How rich and contradictory are the continuities between the two cultures!

The period between his fall from office in 1962 and his retirement from politics in 1968 is a period of gathering storm clouds. The accumulating pressures of the era created economic crises. The failure of dependency economics posed new problems which could not be resolved in the old framework. He acknowledged this pressure for what he called 'more fundamental change,' though I think he had no intuitive feel for it.

His affirmations in 1967 are wholly consistent with the imperatives of his earlier political career:

"I affirm my faith in human freedom, in the right of the people to differ, to criticise. I affirm my hatred of communism and all other forms of political control that deny the basic human rights. I believe in the two party system not because it is ideal, but because it is the only system

19

that can fully guarantee the right of every man to live his own life free from fear and violence. I affirm my faith in the ordinary man, the ordinary Jamaican."

Manley had no trace of colour prejudice in his formation; his affirmation in favour of the ordinary Jamaican was always one in favour of a politics which was regardless of colour. The deep intellectual movement which was to succeed him - the rediscovery of native and African roots which is the story of the cultural revolution of the 1970s - was over the horizon, but not in Manley's sight. The rebirth of Rastafarianism and the cultural nationalism of the 1960s and 1970s were already on the agenda and Manley understood those movements, but they were not and could not be part of his formation.

To the rebellious youth inside and outside the party, whose deep anger and frustration at the slow pace of development was to set the accelerated tempo of the politics of the 1970s, Norman Manley had an old-fashioned message: 'Energy,' he said, 'intelligence and dedication everlasting.'

Fortunately in this period, one of his deep concerns, that of the party succession, was settled with the passage of the leadership of the PNP of his son Michael. But his close relative and arch-rival, the man with whom he had shared the political stage, Alexander Bustamante, had retired in 1968. Manley was not only enormously generous to Bustamante's service to the nation in his farewell speech but he seemed to have an intuitive feel that since the other man had gone it was time for him to go too. He announced his decision not to stand for Party Leader in July 1968. His final address to the PNP Conference was given in 1969 and on the 2nd of September of that year he died, aged 76.

How are we finally to assess this figure who commands so much of the early history of the nation? He was a man of consummate political courage. He gave leadership and example to his nation and people at a critical time of transformation. Some part of that example derived from his secure personal life, in the happy and supportive family life in which he shared; the dedication to his ideals of his family and wife; the special pride that he took in her independent contribution to the artistic and cultural life of Jamaica, the country she adopted, cared for, and in whose heart she has won a special and quite independent place.

His integrity, his probity, was exemplary: a life dedicated to public political service in a time, let me add, increasingly driven by venality, chicanery, double-dealing and the drive for the fast and even more fast disappearing buck. He was the outstanding example in Jamaican politics of a politician around whose name not a whisper of a scandal ever stuck. Only those who understand how close scandal is to the political life of Jamaica will understand what that statement means.

This was a man who, for more than 30 years, right or wrong, put himself at the service of the nation. There is a mistaken view that to understand the political career of men who have played an important role in the history of our time, we have to call for them to be greater than their time, to exhibit universal qualities. Let me share with you my view that people become universal, that is to say their names stand throughout and across time, only because they are equally of their time in their time. Manley therefore was not something else, not some other politician in some other place. He was of his time, of that creole middle class, formed in close association with the continuing educational cultural traditions of the United Kingdom, right or wrong. He never promised to lead the revolution in Jamaica. He never promised the upheaval and upturning of the social structure. If Jamaica needs that, it will have to find its political leadership from some other place.

Does that mean, then, that he played the conventional political role? I want to affirm that he did not. In the history of decolonisation, it has frequently been the case that the progressive middle classes, faced with the danger or threat or promise of independence, of the rising of the political masses to their political rights, have turned round and departed or declined from their progressive commitments and run like hell.

It is Manley's outstanding contribution to have upheld the best of that class to the people, to have insisted that they turn their face towards the progressive line, in facing the problems of autonomy and independence. He gave leadership to his class and, though his class, to the people and, for that reason, to the nation. His career does not require us to overcome or shirk the problems he confronted, the deep legacy and tensions of colonial dependency and the deeper limits of the economic dependency which remain to ravage our people. He was not Superman, but he was, for all that, a man of his time and a leader and founder of the Nation.

Tribute Address by Lord Caradon, Governor of Jamaica, 1951-1957, delivered on the occasion of the First Norman Manley Memorial Lecture

I think I might perhaps first of all say a word about your Chairman's insistence that I am Sir Hugh Foot. I have had a certain amount of trouble with my name. I don't forget an occasion when I was speaking recently in Chicago and the Chairwoman was one of the main supporters of Adlai Stevenson, with whom I had worked closely in the United Nations. In introducing me she said that when she was working with Adlai in the United Nations there was a British ambassador called Sir Hugh Foot. He was a great friend of Adlai and Adlai used to go with him to Jamaica from time to time, but there was nothing that they could do about it. Sometime later, she was in the General Assembly with Adlai when the President of the General Assembly said: "I now call upon the Permanent Representative of the United Kingdom, Lord Caradon, to address the assembly.' And she looked, and said to Adlai, 'You know, funny thing, all these English look the same' (laughter).

I don't want to distract you from what we've just heard. My wife and I are really extremely grateful that you, the organisers of this great meeting, should have invited us to be with you. We wouldn't have missed it. We feel much honoured that we can be with you. And as we listened to that brilliant address by one Rhodes scholar about another, I watched the keenness of your attention. No one moved. No one thought about other than what was being said to us in a very remarkable oration about a very great man. So we are so grateful that we can be with you and we feel it as a privilege that we can share with you the pride of Jamaica, the pride in the men who made modern Jamaica and the pride particularly in Norman Washington Manley. I was thinking as we heard the story of his early life, what magnificent qualifications he had. He was successful in his school. He had taken the prizes in athletics. He had got honours from Oxford and medals from the Army. He was a young man, fortunately for Jamaica, who was brilliantly equipped, together with a wonderful wife, to make his great contribution at a critical time in the history of his country.

I've been fortunate to serve in parts of the world, different parts of the world, in this critical period of the emergence from colonial rule to independence. I have met and known and worked with the leaders in

Africa, in Arabia and in Cyprus. Yes, many remarkable men. And I have known, and very well remember, the privilege of working with Sir Alexander Bustamante too. But I can say that of all those leaders at this critical period (and what happened in this particular period is, I believe, the most important thing that's happened in the whole world. It is the transition from subservience to freedom) if there was one man that I would select who had made the greatest contribution of all, I have no doubt that it would be Norman Manley. And as we gather from his life story, it wasn't just a matter of moving from success to success. In 1944 when he lost the election, with very few seats, it took ten years or more before he came to power in his own country. And I think maybe his greatest contribution was that in those times when he was in the wilderness he was able to keep his people together, to make his contribution to the main purpose, the purpose of independence. And later when he suffered the great set-back, as it was, the great setback of the referendums on West Indian Federation, nothing deterred him from pressing ahead with the purposes which he had set, as we have had described so ably this afternoon.

But I remember him, we remember him, of course, for personal reasons as well as political reasons. What a joy it was to hear him explaining a difficult and complicated matter. Coming to tell me how he was getting on with the negotiations with the bauxite companies. Being able so clearly and so convincingly to speak on any subject. And I often remember it again now, when he came one day to London as the leader of his country and I happened to be in London at the same time. He was to give a radio interview. So I, being in London, eagerly listened to see how he would do. And I realised that he was going to be subject to a great deal of very offensive attack and I felt he could deal with it but at times it got almost intolerable. The questioner said: 'We gather that you were a sergeant in the British Army in the war and that you were refused a commission because of your race.' An insulting thing to say. A disgraceful thing to say. I wondered whether he would be furious and lose his temper. He said: 'I was offered a commission but I was a sergeant in the gunners and I preferred to remain as a sergeant in the gunners.' A wonderful answer for a British audience! Then later I was alarmed to listen as the questioner said: 'But we gather, Mr Manley, that one of the most important matters in your country is the question of population increase, which is very alarming in its speed now, and we gather that you refuse to do anything about it.' I was listening. I was really upset. This was the last question of the interview. And in fact it was the case that Norman Manley had not been prepared to deal with this particular matter. I thought that to end with this question and an unsatisfactory answer would be disastrous. Norman Manley smiled and

23

said: 'Yes, I am a socialist. But you know in matters of relations between the different sexes I believe in private enterprise.' That was it. He finished the whole thing on a cheerful note. Now I give these examples, trivial examples perhaps, but they are examples of his wit, yes, the quickness of his mind. I shall never forget the privilege of being able to work with him, listen to him, privately and politically, and to think that he represented his country so magnificently. And that we can gather together in this remarkable gathering here and listen to a brilliant oration of the kind we had tonight, and that all of us, I believe every one of us in the room, can feel a sense of pride in this national hero. My wife and I are indeed most grateful to you for enabling us to share that experience with you.

The Second Norman Manley Memorial Lecture

Delivered at the Royal Commonwealth Society Hall, Northumberland Avenue, London, on 4 July 1986 by The Hon Vivian Blake, OJ QC. The Chairman of the Proceedings was His Excellency Mr H S Walker, CD, High Commissioner of Jamaica.

"The Pursuit of Excellence"

Since September 1969, the life and work of the late Rt. Excellent Norman Washington Manley have been the topic of countless speeches and a variety of published essays and reviews. Consequently, were our national hero a lesser man, anyone who was asked in this year of grace to make him the subject of yet another commentary would undoubtedly have to wrestle with a serious problem of inspirational bankruptcy. But the many facets of his outstanding and distinguished career have spared me such an ordeal, and he himself has provided the theme for the lecture which I have the honour to deliver tonight.

In his unfinished autobiography, compiled in the first five months of the year in which he died, and speaking of his early youth, he declared:

"I had a real capacity to work hard for what I wanted, and I had an unquenchable belief in excellence. The only superiority I accepted was the superiority of excellence."

This belief was later to become an article of faith. Hard work and the pursuit of excellence dominated his every endeavour, be it as athlete, student, lawyer, political leader or statesman. And yet the attainment of pre-eminence never became an end in itself, achieved solely for the satisfaction of his own ego, but rather was to inure for the benefit of the land and people he loved - in some cases by heightening the aspirations of a developing nation, in other instances by enriching the law and advancing its development, and in other areas by promoting social and economic justice.

I turn then to an examination of a few of the fields in which he distinguished himself and the impact that his achievements had on the Jamaican society. But before I do that, let me confess that I am both a biased witness and a prejudiced judge. I am biased because it was my good fortune when I was called to the Bar in 1948, to read in his Chambers for the greater part of a year. During that time I learnt more about advocacy and the practice of the law than most young barristers manage to learn in a decade. Subsequently, I was his junior in many civil cases, both at first instance and in the Court of Appeal. Later still, I was privileged to appear against him on many occasions. But the association was not exclusively professional. For many years prior to my call to the Bar, I had been drawn into the nationalist movement, which he led, and it was not long before I became very active in the Peoples National Party. This happy combination of common professional interests and political philosophy in turn led to a warm and enduring friendship, which conspires to make me a less than impartial judge. Purist that Manley was, he would be the first to challenge the objectivity of my assessment of the worth of his achievements, and the impartiality of my views as to the effect they had on Jamaica. Be that as it may, I am content to let the facts speak for themselves, and I must leave it to you, Ladies and Gentlemen, to come to your own conclusions as to the weight that should be given to my opinions.

Manley's account of his school days at Jamaica College suggests that his quest for excellence began in earnest at the age of 16, when he decided to make a serious effort to win the Rhodes Scholarship. Perhaps his first outstanding success came in 1912 in the field of sport, when he won the 100 yards event for Jamaica College in the under 19 class at the interscholastic school games. These games took place annually, and athletes from all the country's secondary schools competed. In those days the physiotherapist did not exist. Sprinter's starting blocks had not been invented. Track coaches were unheard of, and such sprinting techniques as existed were largely self-taught. And yet, despite the absence of all these modern-day aids, Manley won the 100 yards sprint in a time of ten seconds. It was a record that was to stand for over a generation, and was only equalled years later by his own son, Douglas, running at the same games for Munro College.

The time of ten seconds for this event ultimately became a landmark in schoolboy athletics and a virtual symbol of sprinting excellence. It set a standard for the generation that was to follow, and a target for successive schoolboy athletes to better. That it fired the imagination of every competitor in the 100 yards event in the many ensuing years, and thereby heightened the standards of competition and performance, cannot be gainsaid.

26

There is another sport with which the Manley name is rarely associated but in which he also achieved excellence. True it was a 'one off' operation, and more a triumph of hard work and application than of natural talent, but this made the feat all the more remarkable - I refer to one particular performance in the game of cricket. Manley's contemporaries record the fact that, as Captain of the Jamaica College cricket eleven that was competing for the Sunlight Cricket Cup, it dawned on him that the team was not likely to succeed without the assistance of at least one good fast bowler. After a futile search for such talent in the upper school, he decided that he had to do the job himself. He had the speed and stride for the run up to the wicket so as to create the necessary momentum for the delivery, and soon mastered the art of bowling the in-swinger, the away-swinger and the yorker. It is said that he even learnt to bowl the occasional bouncer. After six weeks of intensive practice, carried out in the early morning hours before the boarders at Jamaica College had shaken off their slumbers, he was satisfied that he was capable of becoming a devastating opening bowler. And his commitment and efforts were rewarded. That season, he was the most successful fast bowler in Sunlight Cup cricket and Jamaica College duly won the competition. Unfortunately, he has left no record of the formula for his success - not that Jamaica, nor the Westindies, is in need of it, but I believe that at least one set of cricket administrators, not far removed from here, would have benefited from it and, what is more, would have been prepared to offer a king's ransom to obtain it!

It is common knowledge that Manley's schoolboy career culminated with the award to him of the Rhodes Scholarship in 1914, another milestone in the long journey along the road of excellence, and that he left Jamaica later that year for England and Oxford to study law and read for the Bar. According to him: 'The choice of law was an accident. My family talked me into it largely because of my love to talk and argument.'

He was later to caution parents and young people on the threshold of selecting a vocation against the dangers of believing that the capacity to be garrulous necessarily guaranteed success in the legal profession. At Oxford and Gray's Inn, he was an outstanding student. After nearly four years war service which interrupted his studies, he took first class honours in the BCL at Jesus College and was awarded a certificate of honour - the equivalent of a first in the Bar Finals. In the same year in which he sat the Bar Finals, he was the Prizeman at Gray's Inn, in itself a prestigious reward for distinction. He was called to the Bar on the 20th of April 1921, two months short of his 28th birthday, and returned to Jamaica in August 1922 after spending some time in London reading in Chambers as a pupil of the late S C N Goodman, and observing the practice of the English Courts.

His scholastic achievements at Oxford and Gray's Inn were no doubt assisted by the fact that he possessed a prodigious memory. Whilst I was a student in his Chambers, he confided to me that when he took the Bar Finals, he was familiar with the decisions in no less than 1,000 leading cases which he could cite from memory to illustrate important principles in various branches of the law. This was not said as a gesture of idle braggadocio, but rather in a context in which he was bemoaning the fact that, after 26 years of practice, his memory was failing him, and his repertoire - if I may borrow a word from the artistic field - had not kept pace with his student days. To have such a vast storehouse of knowledge at one's fingertips is no mean achievement, and it was a tremendous asset to him in the day-to-day practice of the law. Opinions, which for lesser mortals would require several hours of laborious research involving the need to consult text books and Law Reports on an extensive scale, would be dashed off in a trice. This enabled him virtually to bring the benefits of mass production to his enormous opinion practice without in any way detracting from the quality and standard of his work.

I come now to have a closer look at Manley, the lawyer and advocate. This phase of his career spanned some 33 years, and terminated when he became Chief Minister of Jamaica in 1955 - the year that the Peoples National Party won its first General Election. During that time his fame was legendary, and his name became synonymous with legal skill and expertise.

In the 1920s and indeed as late as 1939, the *Daily Gleaner* would often publish verbatim accounts of the proceedings in the more sensational civil and criminal cases. Manley appeared in nearly all of these. At a time when television was unknown, and radio a luxury which only the privileged could afford, the *Gleaner* was for practical purposes the country's only source of news and the principal medium of entertainment. It was avidly read in the overwhelming majority of middle class homes, and even in some factories where literacy was at a premium workers would contribute a nominal sum from their weekly wages to secure the services of a competent person from outside the business to read the *Gleaner* to them each day as they worked. This was a practice of which the majority of employers approved, not the least because the editorials of those days did not exactly encourage trade union organisation - militant or otherwise. Through these various means, Manley's skill and talent as lawyer and advocate were constantly in the public eye and many of his cases attracted wide attention. In fact, his ability to secure acquittals of those charged with crime, particularly murder, so impressed the simple-minded that it became common for hotheads to threaten: 'Ah will kill you and get Missah

Manley fe get me off.' History does not however record that he was ever called upon to fulfil the prophecy where murder followed such a threat.

For my part, I first became acquainted with the Manley name at the impressionable age of seven or eight when my late father would insist that we take it in turn each night to read the *Gleaner's* Court pages. He was interested primarily in developing my proficiency in reading, but I am convinced that, for good or ill, the experience played a vital part in determining my own choice of profession. But I was in later years to discover how widespread was Manley's reputation for excellence in the field of law.

After leaving secondary school in 1939, I worked in the Jamaica Civil Service and was attached for some years to what was then known as the Labour Department. A Labour Adviser had been seconded from the Colonial Service in 1939 to organise this department. He was Mr Frank Norman. At that time, trade unionism was in its infancy, and there was an urgent need to protect workers from unscrupulous trade union leaders and organisers whose only interest in the movement lay in the collection and diversion of union dues to their own personal use. Accordingly a law was passed requiring all trade unions to register within a certain time after their formation, giving full particulars of their rules, constitution and officers. Unions were also required to file annual dues collected from members. Failure by the officers or organisers to register or file the returns within the specified time, or to account properly for dues collected, was a criminal offence punishable before a resident magistrate, with fine or imprisonment, or both.

Now it transpired in the early 1940s that intensive investigation by the department's officers revealed that a certain trade union leader, now deceased and whose trade union became defunct many years ago, had committed several breaches of the law. The Labour Advisers was of the view that an example should be made of this gentleman so as to deter others of like mind. He therefore recommended to the Colonial Secretary that the Attorney General be asked to institute criminal proceedings and that either the Attorney General, the Solicitor General or some other experienced Law Officer should appear for the Crown.

In due course the prosecution was instituted, but the Labour Adviser's second recommendation went unheeded. An inexperienced Clerk of the Courts prosecuted while Mr N W Manley represented the accused. The outcome was a foregone conclusion, and the alleged culprit was discharged. Subsequently, the Colonial Secretary returned the relevant file to the Labour Adviser for him to note the result of the case. After calling attention in the strongest language to the fact that his recommendation concerning prosecuting counsel had been ignored,

29

a furious Labour Adviser concluded his minute to the Colonial Secretary in these words:

"The appearances in the case and the result of the proceedings are noted. I am not surprised. Suffice it to say that shortly after arriving in Jamaica I had it on good authority that whenever a man in this country gets into trouble, he first flies to Mr Manley, and if Mr Manley is already retained, he next flies to Cuba."

Of course the price that he paid for this legendary reputation was that he was sometimes expected to do the impossible. He very rarely indulged in legal reminiscences, but allow me to share with you an experience which he related to me, the recollection of which caused him some amusement. He had been briefed to represent a young man who was to be tried for the offence of attempted murder in the St Ann's Circuit Court. The depositions which had been taken at the preliminary inquiry revealed that the Crown had an open and shut case. Not only had the complainant been the victim of a savage and murderous attack with a machete, executed by the accused in the presence of several witnesses, but there was abundant evidence that he harboured ill feeling towards the complainant, whom he suspected of having an affair with his concubine. A defence of alibi was out of the question, and so were accident and self defence. There was nothing to suggest that the accused might have been insane at the relevant time. Indeed, the case was so bad that the instructing solicitor was unable to send counsel any statement from the accused indicating any mitigating circumstances.

The trial was to commence at 10am on a Wednesday morning at the St. Ann's Bay Court House before a Judge of the Supreme Court and a jury. Manley had arranged to have a pre-trial conference with his client at 5.30pm on the preceding Tuesday. Unfortunately, on that very day, he was unexpectedly detained in the Kingston Circuit completing another case in which a verdict was not returned until close on to 6pm. There was no means of communicating with his instructing solicitor by telephone to warn of his delayed arrival, and it was no use trying to send a telegram. By the time he left Kingston it was close on to 7pm, and in those days a journey by road to St. Anns Bay would occupy the greater part of three hours. He finally arrived at his instructing solicitor's offices shortly before 10pm. There he found awaiting him not only the solicitor and the accused, but the whole of the accused's family - his father and mother, both in their seventies, an uncle, two sisters, and a brother, all in middle age. So, soon after the introductions were made and greetings were exchanged, Manley put the question that was uppermost in his mind. After briefly referring to the salient features of the case, as revealed by the depositions, he turned to the accused, and asked: "Now what is your defence?" The inquiry was met with a stony silence, which was only broken when the accused's father rose with great dignity, his most disarming smile: 'Barrister, that is what all of we is waiting here for you to tell us.' It is not the function of counsel to fabricate defences for the guilty, as it is commonly believed. And so in the end the accused man was obliged to plead guilty.

Between 1922 and 1931, Manley appeared in numerous civil and criminal cases, both at first instance and in the appellate court. Some of them were sensational, others run of the mill. In 1932, he took silk. This is the highest professional honour that can be conferred on a practising barrister. The right to use the style and title 'King's Counsel,' or 'Queen's Counsel,' dependent on whether the reigning sovereign is male or female, to occupy a place in the inner Bar and to wear a silk gown, is reserved for members of the profession of unimpeachable integrity and character, who have been in practice for at least ten years, and who have achieved distinction in the practice of the law. In pre-independence Jamaica, the honour was conferred by the Governor as the sovereign representative, acting on the recommendation of the Attorney General as official head of the Bar, and the Chief Justice as head of the judiciary. Most barristers then, and even now, practise for at least 15 to 20 years before achieving such distinction and, what is more, make application to the authorities to be considered for appointment. But there are exceptions to every rule. Manley did not apply for silk. He was invited to take silk. Further the honour was conferred on him when he had been in practice two months short of the usual period of ten years. No other barrister in Jamaica has taken silk so early.

Between 1932 and 1955 Manley became the undisputed leader of the Jamaican Bar and the dominant figure in the legal profession. He appeared in all the important cases, civil or criminal, that came to trial. Whenever litigation threatened, there was a mad rush to retain his services. Whilst the unsucessful did not always fly to Cuba, many of them preferred to seek settlements rather than run the risk of incurring costs in law suits in which he was on the other side. During this period, he travelled to England where he successfully defended one of our countrymen charged with murder, and also made history as the first Jamaican barrister to appear before the Judicial Committee of the Privy Council.

I will not attempt to discuss his many outstanding cases. Apart from the accounts of some of them which are to be found in the old newspapers kept by the Institute of Jamaica, no permanent public record of them has been preserved. Unfortunately, we are, as a people, yet to develop a heightened sense of the importance of our own history, and my hope is that one day in the not-too-distant future, some diligent and

31

enterprising young lawyer will do the necessary research and undertake the publication of a book dedicated to 'Norman Manley - Lawyer and Advocate,' in which these cases will find a place. Manley was not given to frequent discussion of his court appearances. Unlike most good advocates, and contrary to general opinion, he was no egotist. He himself declared:

"Nearly all good advocates are happy talking about their cases. In ten years I was to discover how strong the habit could be, and I decided for myself that in my private life I would keep out, really keep out, talk about law and cases. And I did."

So, Ladies and Gentlemen, such knowledge as I have of his cases is based on second-hand information and my own recollection. And I will mention some of them in passing, not to regale you with their detail, but merely to illustrate his legal attributes and the forensic skills in which he excelled.

The aim of the advocate is to persuade his audience, be it judge or jury, to agree with his particular contention concerning facts and situations. For this purpose he may have to deal with many things. Benjamin Disraeli, who was in his time a master of argument, once described the good advocate as one who was able 'to illustrate the obvious, elaborate the self-evident, and expatiate on the common place.'

The obvious is very often obscured by prejudice. The self-evident is sometimes blurred by mental intransigence. And, precisely because commonsense is not common, the commonplace frequently requires careful discussion. The means by which the advocate seeks to overcome these barriers, and achieve his objective, is the use of words. The great advocate never indulges in empty histrionics. Theatrics are no answer to seemingly unfavourable evidence. Neither is he an orator pure and simple. The silver-tongued orator succeeds only in convincing his followers. He does not convert the sceptic, nor win over the hesitant. What is more, in a court of law, the advocate frequently has to grapple with pre-conceived notions and ideas and, as one writer so aptly puts it, 'Against these oratory merely bombinates in the void.'

What then, you may ask, is the instrument which the truly great advocate employs in the performance of his task? I would answer with the words of the distinguished author Gerald Abrahams, who, in his book, *The Legal Mind,* states:

"It is the eloquence that flows essentially from thought, interspersed with the occasional ornamental phrase, or literary allusion. It is the language of the man who knows what he is saying; who is confident in his ability to find the right words for the ideas he wishes to express; who can state and drive home point after point, with due deliberation at a pace which his audience can follow; who is so fluent that he is

32

never lost for words, and can start and complete his sentences without deviation - above all, whose speech is distinguished for its simplicity and clarity, and who is so sensitive to his surroundings as to be instinctively aware of the impression he is making on his audience."

Those of us who were privileged to hear Norman Manley address a court of law, or speak on radio or television, or at conferences of the Peoples National Party, will, I am confident, have little difficulty in recognising this as an accurate description of his compelling and persuasive style. And irrespective of his audience, it remained basically the same. He was first and last the great persuader, appealing primarily to reason and intellect, and rarely, if ever, pandering to the emotions. He did not come by that style by accident, neither could it be regarded as a natural gift. It was the product of experience and observation, aided by a vocabulary that had been enriched by extensive reading.

I wish I could illustrate that eloquence by reference to a closing address which Manley made to a jury, or to an argument which he advanced in the Court of Appeal. But I am without the requisite source material. Nonetheless, some examples, chosen at random from his many other speeches, will suffice to demonstrate his style. On the extent to which the old imperialist system frustrated creative expression and demeaned a subject people (the year was 1938) he had this to say:

"The dead hand of imperialism is made manifest in the dearth of our culture, in the paucity and poverty of our arts, in the drying up of the sources of charity, in the decay of faith and the licentiousness of morals, in the dishonesty of our escapism, in the malice of our leaders, in the cowardice of government, in the narrow mean circumspection of all our horizons. One touch of creative intensity and a veritable desert would quicken into life with rank weeds jostling the flower shoots, striving for living room. There would be life and trouble, blossom and fruit, but the dead hand, quietly with blind efficiency, closes on it all."

Observe the central thought, the fluency of the language, and the ability to state point after point in condemnation of imperialism, compelling the audience to the inescapable conclusion that is was a totally suffocating phenomenon.

In different vein is a passage from a speech made to the members of the Philadelphia Bar Association in 1967. Here Manley discusses Jamaica's aims in relation to the attainment of racial harmony, and defines the fundamental prerequisite of true racial integration with eloquent simplicity:

"We do not seek mere tolerance between people of different races and admixtures. What we aim at is a society in which the races of mankind live together in mutual harmony and respect and affection, where the value of a person has nothing at all to do with his race or the colour of his skin. In a word we press on to the end where colour has ceased to have any psychological significance in society.

"Let me make this clear - a society which still talks about racial tolerance has not yet reached or is barely at the first stage of the process of racial integration. No society will achieve the true goal until colour ceases to have psychological importance in the mind of the society itself. It may take decades, it may take a thousand years, but the world will not be civilised until that goal is finally achieved."

A painful reminder of how barbarous is that distant regime which those who dither now about sanctions unwittingly support.

So much then for his eloquence in addressing a court, be his audience judge or jury. But there were other branches of advocacy in which he excelled. I begin with his skill and effectiveness as a cross-examiner. Cross-examination is not an argument conducted with a witness. Neither is it a collection of miniature speeches addressed to him. On the contrary, as Abrahams says, it is, or ought to be, a succession of well planned questions designed firstly to bring evidence before the court, secondly to expose falsehood and inaccuracy, and lastly to throw light on testimony that has already been given. It does not mean asking questions in heat or temper, but, when properly conducted, is a calm and detached, yet devastatingly effective exercise. To be successful, the cross-examiner must have a full grasp of the facts of the case and the evidence that has been given. He needs also to have human understanding and a little subtlety. Excellence in this branch of advocacy requires hard work. The material in counsel's brief must be studied and mastered, and serious thought given to the questions that should be put to the particular witnesses. Any cross-examination that is conducted in a haphazard way, and as a hit and miss operation, will have disastrous consequences for the cross-examiner and his unfortunate client.

Manley never failed to master the facts of the cases he was engaged in, and his retentive memory was an asset in enabling him to keep abreast of the evidence that had been given. He was very skilled in the subtle use of the material at his disposal and he had a great understanding of human behaviour, its strengths and weaknesses.

Manley was also adept at leading unfavourable witnesses into exaggerations so gross as to be destructive of their own credibility - as for instance witnesses in running-down cases, who frequently saw motor cars travelling like greased lighting down mean and narrow Jamaican country lanes, and who could very easily be led to say that, although the speed was not as fast as 150 miles per hour, it was certainly not less than 95-100 miles per hour.

But the cases in which he was the cross-examiner par excellence were those which involved some technical or scientific subject matter. He invariably made himself a master in the relevant field before a case began, and this coupled with his extensive general knowledge and grasp of scientific matters, often made him more of an expert on the day than the experts he cross-examined. When in the early 1950s he defended Beard, the young Jamaican who was charged with murder before an English court, it was his expertise in the field of forensic medicine that enabled him to establish in cross-examination of the pathologist that the fatal wounds could not have been inflicted by a left-handed man such as the accused, but were delivered by a person who was right-handed. *Rex v. Alexander* and *Wehby* [1931], a murder case which became a case *celebre*, it was his dominance in the realm of ballistics that demonstrated decisively that the markings on the fatal bullet which the expert swore were peculiar to bullets fired from Wehby's revolver, were not marks of identification at all, but were common to bullets fired from revolvers of similar age and make.

It is not without significance that one of Manley's favourite quotations was the ancient adage, 'The race is not for the swift, nor the battle for the strong, but for him that endureth to the end.'

It was indeed symbolic of his own patience and stamina. Until he was 70 years of age, he could put in 15-16 hours of concentrated work each day without difficulty. Between 1944 and 1955, his political involvement made serious demands on his time, but his legal work did not suffer as a result. If anything his work day just became a little longer. On a typical Sunday during those years he would spend the entire morning working in the Supreme Court Library in downtown Kingston, and be off by lunch time to various rural areas to address political rallies and meetings. Very rarely would he return to his home at Drumblair before 11pm if, as was often the case, he was engaged in a witness action on the following Monday, he would study his brief on his return home. During this period, I well recall being required as his junior to attend pre-trial conferences at Drumblair which began at midnight, and ended at anything between 2.30 and 3am. And I can never forget that on one particular occasion, when a conference ended at 3am, I was asked to accompany him to a cowshed some considerable distance from the house and hold a torch whilst he inspected two sick calves.

It was stamina coupled with his great patience that enabled him, assisted by the late Mr Aston Simpson, solicitor, and Dr Ludlow Moody, to spend endless nights and countless hours firing rounds of ammunition from a Colt revolver into a tank of water subjecting each bullet recovered to microscopic examination until at last they reproduced a bullet with markings identical with those which the expert in the Alexander murder case had sworn could only have been produced by the accused's firearm. And it was that capacity to strive against odds, and be resolute in commitment, which won the praise of the Honourable Mr Justice Adrian Clarke, who presided over that trial. After the jury returned their verdict of acquittal, he felt constrained to tell the accused before discharging them:

"You have been most fortunate in your choice of counsel. Genius is the capacity to take infinite pains and Mr Manley has amply demonstrated that quality in his conduct of your defence."

This was not the first, neither was it to be the last, time that Manley's ability was the subject of favourable judicial comment.

Then in 1949 or thereabouts, there was the famous case of *The Karsote Co., v. The Vick Chemical Company*. Vick had for years sold a product under the name 'Vaporub,' which was reputed to be efficacious in the treatment of respiratory ailments. Karsote sought to market a product under a similar name and the Vick company promptly sued for infringement of their trade mark. They said that the word 'Vaporub' was an invented word which had for years been associated with their product and that, in the trade and to the buying public, the words 'Vicks' and 'Vaporub' had become synonymous. Manley was counsel for the Vick Company. Sir Lennox O'Reilly, KC, then the doyen of the Trinidad Bar, came to Jamaica to represent Karsote. At the hearing, Mr Justice Savary rejected Vick's claim and found for Karsote, but the Court of Appeal reversed his decision and gave judgement for Vick. Karsote thereupon appealed to the Privy Council.

Now trade mark law is a highly specialised subject of extreme nicety. In those days a trade mark case rarely, if ever, reached the Court in Jamaica, and it was not a branch of the law with which Manley could claim day to day familiarity. The case was of the utmost importance to the Vick Company because, were they to lose, their right to exclusive use of the name 'Vaporub' throughout the world would be destroyed. And Vaporub was then their largest money earner. Karsote selected as their counsel for the appeal two of the most eminent silks at the English Bar who specialised in trade mark work. One of them was I believe Upjohn KC, later to become Lord Upjohn, and a Lord of Appeal in Ordinary. But the Vick Company had so much faith and confidence in Manley's ability that they ignored the remainder of the distinguished specialists at the English Bar and retained Manley to appear for them. The rest is history. Despite the able arguments of Karsote's counsel, and the initial opposition of the Bench, Manley read them a lesson in the intricacies of the subject and he prevailed. Vick's confidence was vindicated and their trade mark was preserved. This, to my mind, was the supreme triumph of Manley the lawyer. One of the Law Lords who was a member of the Court which heard the appeal is reputed to have openly told the member of his Inn, whilst dining in Hall, that the best argument that had ever been presented to the Law Lords in his time on a point of trade mark law had been advanced by a colonial barrister by the name of Manley!

No account of Manley's role as lawyer and advocate would be complete without a passing reference to his wit - an indispensable weapon in the armoury of any able counsel. The Bench everywhere is always characterised by the presence of one or two petty tyrants, whose excesses and overbearing conduct are best curbed by effective repartee. He was not as abrasive as F E Smith who later as Lord Birkenhead became Lord Chancellor of England in 1919. In his days at the Bar, 'F E' silenced many an irascible member of the Bench by his scathing retorts. On one occasion he was obliged to rebuke a talkative judge for making a most improper remark in the presence of a jury which was gravely prejudicial to a defendant for whom he appeared. The judge took exception to the rebuke and, raising his voice, said: 'Now Mr Smith, you are being most offensive.' Quick as a flash, the reply was: 'That I know my Lord, but whereas I am trying to be, your Lordship just cannot help it.'

Manley could however use sardonic humour to great effect when the situation warranted it. I was with him on one occasion in the Court of Appeal when he was arguing a case in which the appellant had been convicted of the offence of manufacturing gin illicitly in breach of the Excise Laws. Manley's submission was that the Crown had failed to prove that the liquid found in the still was gin. One of the Judges of Appeal, known in the profession as a well known tippler, and who was notorious for condemning all things Jamaican, interjected: 'But Mr Manley, even the abominable stuff which is locally manufactured under proper authority is difficult to recognise as gin.' To the amusement of the entire Court, including the other two members of the Bench, Manley replied: 'Your Honour has the advantage, and I must bow to your superior knowledge.'

And then there was the other Justice of Appeal who sought to silence a plea that a sentence of imprisonment for a first offence was manifestly excessive and ought to be replaced by a probation order, by remarking: 'That approach is no doubt sound in a civilised country,' implying of course that Jamaica was not. This aroused Manley's indignation and evoked the response: 'My submission is based on the practice of civilised judges who administer the law in a civilised way.'

You may at this stage be tempted to inquire what were his weaknesses. As a lawyer and advocate, he was difficult to fault. But like all human beings he had his imperfections. It was inevitable that shoddy work should be anathema to one who was so deeply committed to the achievement of excellence. Equally, it was not surprising that so industrious a man should be impatient with indolence. And as it was relatively easy for him to achieve distinction in his many endeavours, he did not suffer fools gladly. And so he could be especially hard on the incompetent, the lazy, and the stupid. But rather than condemn these shortcomings, I would prefer to echo Goldsmith's immortal lines: 'We must touch his weaknesses with a delicate hand. There are some faults so nearly allied to excellence, that we can scarce weed out the fault without eradicating the virtue.'

This brings me, Ladies and Gentlemen, to the end of my review of Manley's pursuit of excellence in his capacity as advocate and lawyer. There is a tendency for most Jamaicans to view this aspect of his career as marking only the brilliance of the pleader's skills and the triumph of legal erudition. But this is to overlook the immense contribution that he made to the development of the law by the quality of his arguments before the appellate and other courts. It is a well-worn truism that the Bench is as strong as the Bar that argues before it, and many of the landmark decisions which are to be found in the Jamaica Law Reports between 1932 and 1955, and in most of which he played a dominant role, testify to this self-evident fact.

Even though he won their grudging respect, Manley was often an object of envy and jealously to those of his immediate legal contemporaries who had to appear against him in the courts. But to the younger generation of barristers who came to the Bar shortly after the second world war, he became a father figure, admired, respected and, above all, to be emulated. He could always find time to help a puzzled colleague solve a knotty legal problem, was very generous with helpful advice, and always ready to put work the way of the struggling junior. His encouragement and example were powerful catalysts in bringing to birth the strong Bar for which Jamaica became noted in the period between 1955 and 1962, and which in turn provided the leaven for the outstanding Bar of the post-independence period. For much of this, credit is due to him.

Towards the end of his legal career, he began to grow tired of the practice of the law. It was not sufficiently creative, and its attractions began to wane. He himself wrote: 'Law and Court work did not absorb all my mental energy. I even found law a largely formal matter with wide areas of dry insignificance.'

By that time he had become deeply involved in politics and almost preoccupied with Jamaica's pressing social and economic problems. Perhaps, like that master of satire, Anatole France, he was beginning to look askance at the majestic egalitarianism of a system of law which made it a criminal office for rich and poor alike to beg in the street or steal bread. It is clear, however, that he was starting to make common cause with Cicero in believing that the good of his people was the chief law. And when he became Chief Minister in 1955, it was not surprising that he described the task to which he had set himself as taking up the brief for the people of Jamaica.

In the years that followed, Manley wholeheartedly devoted all his legal acumen and ability to the promotion of the country's welfare. The plight of the Jamaican small farmer, whose title to his plot of land rested almost entirely on possession, was one of his earliest concerns. Banks and other lending institutions had for years been reluctant to lend money to this group of disadvantaged persons because of their inability to furnish good title as security for the loan. The cost of obtaining registered titles was prohibitive for the poor and the process was extremely slow. In the result, small farmers were unable to obtain the necessary finance to enable them to develop their plots and much fertile land was rendered either idle, or under utilised. Past governments had tried in vain to solve the difficulty - but Manley was not to be defeated. He fell back on his legal resources and recalled that, under an early 19th Century Jamaican stature, which had long been repealed, anyone who held his land for seven years in good faith under a deed or will, acquired a title to the land which was good against the whole world, provided he had improved it during the period. And out of this, the idea for The Facilities for Titles Law was born. It was Manley's brainchild, and it became law in October 1955. Under its provisions, any person who could prove undisturbed possession of land for seven continuous years was entitled to apply for a loan for defined purposes and, once he had obtained it, the fact of obtaining the loan conferred an irrevocable title for the benefit of himself and his lender. Here was a classic example of a law created for the purpose of economic improvement which, but for the excellence of legal acumen, would never have been conceived.

This was followed by the re-negotiation of the agreement with the bauxite companies which were operating in the country. At that time, Jamaica was almost the largest bauxite producer in the world, but under the arrangements with the previous administration. Reynolds, Kaiser, and Alumina Jamaica Limited were paying the Government a mere pittance to mine and export ore. Manley's professional skills as a lawyer, and his understanding of the complexities of American, Canadian, and Jamaican tax laws, enabled him to secure an agreement under which the rate of royalty and income tax paid by the companies for each ton of bauxite mined was increased buy over 500 per cent. This provided a welcome boost to the country's revenue. Another instance of legal excellence operating for social and economic improvement!

Perhaps the most outstanding example of his innovative legal genius was the Beach Control Law. From the end of the Second World War and continuing well into the 1950s, there had been a dramatic growth in tourism. Hotel construction expanded, particularly on the north coast and in the eastern parishes. There was a boom in land sales. Many hitherto quiet fishing villages were transformed overnight into tourist resorts, and villas and apartments sprang up in many coastal areas. There was a grave danger that the majority of Jamaica's best beaches would in time become the exclusive preserve of holiday makers from abroad and the privileged few. Many fishermen, who had for generations used particular beaches for putting to sea and mooring their boats, were threatened with eviction and loss of livelihood when the adjoining land passed into foreign hands. Unless some means could be found to protect the fishermen and secure to the people of Jamaica at large right of access to their beaches and sea, they would be deprived of one of the country's finest amenities.

The situation came to a head during Manley's term of office as Chief Minister between 1955 and 1962. Interested citizens' groups suggested different solutions. Government opinion on the matter was divided. Basically, there were two schools of thought. One view was that the government should use its powers under existing law and from time to time compulsorily acquire beach sites throughout the island for public use. This of course would involve the payment of substantial compensation and be a drain on the country's limited finances. The other school wanted legislation to make the purchase of sea-front land subject to governmental approval, and also to regulate the use of existing hotel beaches, so as to guarantee a right of access to the public. This latter proposal was defective in that it failed altogether to address the problem of such beach sites as had already been acquired. Besides, any unsophisticated attempt to use raw power and political muscle to interfere with hotelier's rights was likely to be counterproductive, especially at a time when every effort was being made to attract foreign investment.

Neither view found favour with Manley. After much thought, he hit upon a brilliant idea which was to be the lever which the government would use to control the use of beaches in the public interest. It had the salutary virtue that the claim to exercise this control was to be based on the government's possession of an unimpeachable property right.

Now a beach site is hardly of any use to its owner unless it can afford unmolested access to the open sea. Consequently, whoever owned or controlled the sea shore could effectively prevent the owner of the adjoining land and his guests from reaching the open sea, or alternatively extract a price from them for the privilege of passing and re-passing over this area of land on their way out to deeper water. By legal definition, the sea shore, or foreshore as it is sometimes called, is that portion of the land which lies between the high water mark of the ordinary tides and the low water mark. And it is, and was always, well settled law that sea shore or foreshore is vested in and belongs to the Crown, save where it has been granted to the subject. But because the difference between the high tide and low tides in Jamaica is almost imperceptible, nearly everyone had forgotten about the existence of sea shore of foreshore as a separate and distinct entity of land. And apart from Manley, those who remembered it failed to recognise the significance of its ownership in the solution of the problem that had arisen. In fact, all and sundry had assumed that ownership of land adjoining the beach automatically carried with it a right of free access to the open sea.

It was in those circumstances and against this background that Manley devised the Beach Control Law. Based on the Crown's unquestioned right to legal ownership of the sea shore, the owners of all hotels and other sites adjoining the sea who used, or proposed to use their premises to afford sea bathing or other aquatic facilities to a class of the public, were required to obtain a licence so to do from an authority specially appointed for the purpose. The authority had power to refuse an application, or to grant licences upon special terms, including terms which ensured that members of the public other than the licensee's paying guests had rights of access to the sea for the purposes of bathing. The law also made provision for the preservation, protection and regulation of fishing rights, and the use of beaches as mooring places for boats. At the time of its passage, the Beach Control Law was unique in the Caribbean and, as far as I am aware, it still is in the English-speaking developing world. It stands not only as a memorial to the ingenuity of its creator, but as a symbol of legal excellence.

I do not pause to trouble you with the details of other statues passed whilst Manley was head of the elected government which owe their form and content to his incisive mind, and all of which were designed to achieve social and economic change. His final contribution was the Independence Constitution of 1962, which was prepared under his guidance. He was well aware of its limitations, but through its provisions he helped to bequeath to the young nation the framework within which good government could be maintained and human rights could be preserved. Realist that he was, he recognised that in the end the Constitution would be what the government and the people chose to make of it. But it remained his fervent hope that, in its interpretation, its invigorating spirit would always take precedence over narrow and pedantic legalism.

Mr. Chairman, Ladies and Gentlemen, this is but an inadequate account of Norman Manley's lifelong pursuit of excellence. Those of us whose lives were touched by his, learnt from him the importance of industry, the virtues of patience, and the dynamic of commitment. And long before he died, all this together with the brilliance of his achievements, combined to make the Jamaicans of my generation see him, albeit for different reasons, in the same way as Juliet saw her Romeo. And like her, we too could say:

When he shall die,
Take him and cut him out in little stars
And he will make the face of heaven so fine
That all the world will be in love with night,
And pay no worship to the garish sun.

So let us keep his memory evergreen, that his example may live forever.

The Third Norman Manley Memorial Lecture

*Given by the Commonwealth Secretary General Sir Shridath S
Ramphal at The Royal Commonwealth Society on 24 June 1988*

"No Island
is an Island"

The first two lectures in this series which commemorate the
life and work of one of the greatest Westindians, Norman
Washington Manley, were concerned with Manley and
Jamaica. In honouring me the invitation to deliver the Third
Memorial Lecture you have specifically asked me to cast
the net of analysis and reminiscence somewhat wider and to speak on
the theme of the Caribbean or, as I would prefer to say, the Westindies.
It is a theme, of course, that was central to Norman Manley's life and
work. Indeed, it was in his role of a committed believer in Westindian
unity that I first came under Manley's spell. He was the first Westindian
politician to move and inspire me in that cause, and it was here in
London, at the LSE, during one of his visits in the early 1950s. The
preparatory work on West Indian Federation was gathering momentum
and Manley shared with us - some of the generation that would play a
part in its unfolding - his vision of the future Westindian Nation. It is a
vision I have never lost nor lost faith in. I was to see, and work, with
Norman Manley in the coming years through the increasingly intensive
Westindian conferences leading to the establishment of the Federation
in 1957; conferences in which he played such a leading role.

My next reminiscence of 'N W' is very different. It was ten years
later, in 1964; the federal experiment was over: Jamaica was independent
and Norman Manley was in opposition. The dream we had shared and
which he had tried so hard to make come true - the dream of Westindian
nationhood - lay shattered. The Federation of the West Indies which I
too had worked to bring to independence had been dissolved on the
very day - 31 May, 1962 - that had been agreed upon, at the last

Westindian Conference Norman Manley attended (May/June 1961), as the date for the establishment of the Westindian Nation.

I was the Assistant Attorney-General of the Federation and involved in drafting what was to be the Independence Constitution. We were half way through when the referendum in Jamaica answered 'No' to Federation and, as it was to transpire, to Norman Manley. I left Port of Spain, until then the Federal capital, on 30 August 1962, the day before Trinidad and Tobago's Independence and 24 days after Jamaica's. I left for Harvard on a Guggenheim Fellowship where I would reflect and write on the prospects for the Caribbean - no longer the Westindies.

Looking back on it all now, did the acute disappointment which I felt border on petulance? Perhaps it did, but let it be said that we had been stirred by a loftier vision of nationhood than that which independence on an island basis seemed to offer: a vision of one Westindian nation, not one of the 12 that did emerge. After Harvard, I joined my friend and former colleague, Harvey DaCosta, who had been Federal Attorney General, in law practice in Jamaica. My name-plate, I am glad to say, is still there at 20½ Duke Street, Kingston. It was in practice that I last encountered Norman Manley. He, too, had returned to the Bar, although he did only opinion work. He was a revered figure at the Bar, but caused more than a little concern among his younger colleagues by adhering resolutely to the low level fees he had been accustomed to year earlier. Since he was 'N W', his fees were the bench-mark for us. But let me turn, as you have asked, to the Caribbean.

"The islands are separated by miles of sea and to a close and more territorial political union it may be said 'opposuit natura'." So concluded Walwyn Shepherd in 1900, writing of the Westindies in the *Journal of Comparative Legislation*. In other words, as the 20th Century dawned, nature itself seemed to say 'No' to Westindian nationhood. Some 63 years later, writing in '*Foreign Affairs*' just after Jamaica and Trinidad and Tobago had become independent, Philip Sherlock had to say:

"Division is the heritage of the Caribbean. The separateness of the islands in the archipelago that curves for a thousand miles from the tip of Florida to the mouth of the Orinoco is reflected in the fact that they have no common name. Each island shares with the others the same startling beauty of sun-drenched mountains and peacock seas; each has the same social configuration resulting from the same techniques of production, the intensive cultivation of one crop, and slavery. Yet the keynote is contrast, the dominant theme competition. The rivalries of Western Europe broke the region into segments, each tightly integrated into the trading system of the metropolitan power, sealed off in an almost watertight compartment and stocked with people brought together from Europe, a score of West African Kingdoms and the central

44

provinces of India. Nowhere else in the New World is there so sharp a juxtaposition of different races, languages, religions - different legal, educational and political systems."

In 1975, in my last speech in the Caribbean before coming to London as Commonwealth Secretary-General, a speech I called 'To Care for CariCom', I myself said this:

"A consequence of our relative success over the last ten years is a readiness to believe that unity is our natural state - one which will subsist despite ourselves. It is a dangerous falsehood. A history of colonialism and the geography of a scattered archipelago deny its validity. The natural state of our Caribbean is fragmentation; without constant effort, without unrelenting perseverance and discipline in suppressing instincts born of tradition and environment, it is to our natural state of disunity that we shall return."

Yet there is another side that is unifying and it, too, is part of our natural state and our heritage. It is the unmistakable, unchanging fact of a Westindian identity. Over 250 years ago, in 1722, Pere Labat, writing about his travels among the islands and states, invoked that identity, so palpable to him, in support of the common destiny to which he saw us all committed as part of an even wider Caribbean. He wrote:

"I have travelled everywhere in your sea of the Caribbean from Haiti to Barbados, to Martinique and Guadeloupe, and I know what I am speaking about ... You are all together, in the same boat, sailing on the same uncertain sea ... citizenship and race unimportant, feeble little labels compared to the message that my spirit brings to me: that of the position and predicament which history has imposed upon you ... I saw it first with the dance ... the merengue in Haiti, the beguine in Martinique and today I hear, *de mon oreille morte*, the echo of calypsos from Trinidad, Jamaica, St Lucia, Antigua, Dominica and the legendary Guiana ... It is no accident that the sea which separates your lands makes no difference to the rhythm of your body."

In many ways, the two and a half centuries since Labat sailed the Caribbean should have strengthened both the reality and the awareness of a common identity and developed among our people an instinct for unity. The shared experience of bondage that slavery and indenture imposed, the common experience of colonialism and, in later years, of struggle for release from it, compel a sense of community. An almost identical environment, propitious to the flowering of the cultural traditions of its transported people ensures a socio-cultural unity. Joint patterns of colonial administration result in a uniform legal-political framework; transmitted traditions of the rule of law and of parliamentary democracy are part of a Westindian ethos. How natural, then, is our state of disunity, how real our heritage of division?

Perhaps we need to look back before we can look forward with confidence. Let me try to do so by recalling two episodes in our constitutional cross-stitch of the Leewards and Windwards Islands - today's OECS countries - who are once again exploring the ways of political unity: different people of a different age renewing the effort to overcome the vicissitudes of smallness by building bridges across a dividing sea.

By the 1660s English settlements had been established in St Christopher, Barbados, Nevis, Antigua and Montserrat: all of them - 'the Caribee Islands' - came under the executive authority of a common Governor-in-Chief stationed at Barbados. In the beginning, there was union. But the marriage was unpopular with the planters of the islands other than Barbados and, through political pressure locally and representations in London, a separation was arranged. In 1671, a special Commission was issued appointing Sir Charles Wheeler "Governor-in-Chief over St Christopher, Nevis, Montserrat, Antigua, Barbuda, Anguilla and all other Leeward Islands which His Majesty has seen fit to separate from the Government of Barbados." Thus began the long series of island configurations, groupings and re-groupings, unions and federations and confederations, which were to characterise constitutional developments in the Westindies for nearly 300 years.

Peace in Europe after 1815 ushered in a period of calm in the Westindies and Whitehall could give more attention to the problems of government in the Caribbee Islands. In 1816, the experiment was tried of dividing the Leewards into two groups under separate governors, but in 1833 as part of a more general policy of consolidation, the islands were again united under a common governor, with Dominica, which had been a separate colony since 1770, added to the group. However, the need which had prompted even earlier attempts at federalism in the 17th Century persisted and, in 1869, the Colonial Office, inspired by Canada's efforts two years earlier, became the champion of federalism in the Leewards. Sir Benjamin Pine was appointed Governor with a mandate "to form these islands into one colony, with one Governor, one Superior Court and one Corps of Police": a formula for union not so unlike that currently being advanced by some OECS leaders. But Pine was soon to discover that even the most modest alteration in the status quo presented innumerable difficulties. "It must be remembered," he wrote, "that these islands, small and insignificant as they may be, have for centuries possessed forms of government not only wholly unsuited to the times when they were founded, but which while ceasing to be applicable to present circumstances have kept up among the ruling classes a spirit of self-importance and narrow patriotism which may seem ludicrous but cannot be ignored." Note that reference to 'ruling classes'; it has its present-day resonances.

The greatest obstacle to agreement was the proposal for a common treasury: "What! they say", reported Pine on the attitude of the planters of St Kitts, "shall the rich and prosperous island of St Kitts share its overflowing treasury with the bankrupt island of Antigua?" Alexander Bustamante was to say as much at the Montego Bay Conference in 1947 - three-quarters of a century later - when he described 98 per cent of the other islands as "pauperised and in a state of bankruptcy." "I have never heard", he protested, "that in going with bankrupts one can become successful or prosperous." This time St Kitts was among the bankrupts. Faced with an almost unanimous opposition from the islands, the Secretary of State was forced to abandon that 19th Century plan of union in favour of federation, though for a time he remained adamant over the strength of the central authority. When, after 18 months of negotiation, Pine obtained the approval of the island legislatures, it was to a federal union far removed from Whitehall's earlier plans.

A former President of Nevis once described the resulting Leeward Islands Federation as "a government powerless in itself to do good, but which has developed great capacities for hindering any good being done by the several parts." Yet it limped along until 'defederation' in 1957 as a prelude to the more inclusive federal union. No less than 300 years had been spent in a contest between rationality and pettiness with the latter consistently triumphant.

In the Windwards, meanwhile, the same forces were at work. The Peace of Paris in 1763 had brought a temporary lull to Anglo-French conflict in the Caribbean, and Grenada, with the little Grenadines attached, St Vincent, Dominica and Tobago were ceded to Great Britain. Grouped together as the 'Southern Caribbee Islands' they were immediately formed into one government at Grenada. Once again, in the beginning, there was union. The experiment, however, was short-lived. In 1771, Dominica was separated and placed under a separate governorship. In 1776, St Vincent followed suit. When in 1783, Tobago was ceded to the French by the Treaty of Versailles the union had ended by elimination.

Until the Treaty of Paris in 1814 was it finally decided that the English, and not the French, were to be responsible for the Windwards. All four of the "Southern Caribee Islands" were returned to Great Britain, with the addition of St Lucia, but no attempt was made to revive the former union.

Pine's moderate success in the 1870s in securing the federation of the Leeward Islands encouraged the Colonial Office to hope for similar developments in the Windwards and, in 1871, Governor Rawson was instructed along such lines: "As you have been aware from the time of your appointment as Governor," wrote the Secretary of State to him some time later, "Her Majesty's Government are anxious that the islands of the Windward group should be federated under a stronger and more efficient system of administration than can be secured to each of them while they continue separate." Far from convinced himself of the wisdom of 'confederation' - as the proposal was referred to in the Windwards - and certain of the opposition of the legislatures in Barbados, Grenada and Tobago, he recommended that it should be preceded by the conversion of the now 'representative' legislatures into single chambers, in which the Crown would have power to bring in united action. But if 'confederation' was distasteful to the island legislatures, confederation on the basis of Crown Colony Government was an absolute anathema. In the minds of the planters - remember, it was still only the planters - the issues became intermingled: once that had occurred, the fate of 'confederation' was sealed. Rawson's successor, J Pope Hennessy, eventually proposed a 'scheme for administrative confederation' which amounted to little more than a six-point programme for the creation of certain common public institutions financed by the islands of the Windward group, including Barbados.

In the smaller islands the proposals were favourably received, but in Barbados by this time the very mention of the word 'confederation' had become the signal for political agitation. The opposition of the planters hardened and became organised and at the same time there arose a more widely held fear and distrust of 'confederation' - a situation, in Pope Hennessy's view, deliberately created by the systematic misrepresentation of the proposals by their enemies. Local demonstrations grew into riots and there was talk of landing troops to maintain the peace. Proposals from Pope Hennessy for reform in the system of land tenure ensured his popularity with the planters who petitioned the Secretary of State for his recall. Towards the end of the same year Pope Hennessy was promoted to Hong Kong. Rationality had not triumphed in the Windwards either.

A congenial parochialism; a fear on the part of the wealthier islands of having to carry their weaker associates; a sense of security in entrenched power; all contributed to form an effective resistance at this level. At the heart of this was the fact that the 'old representative system,' which traditionally has been regarded as a proud inheritance, and which, in the islands, in many cases preceded the establishment of Crown Colony Government, was truly representative in little more than name. As late as 1876 in Barbados the Lower House was returned by an electorate of 1,000 out of a population of 180,000.

There clearly has not been any ordered constitutional progress towards political unity. Yet it is undeniable that from the very beginnings of a British influence in the Caribbean there has been a centripetal force steadily driving these territories together. The source of the energy has not always been the same. In the 17th and early 18th Centuries, a period of constant struggle for supremacy of metropolitan authority, it derived from the need for greater efficiency and economy in the administration of the territories and its impetus came from those responsible for their administration. This need remained, but the 20th Century has ended a new and more dynamic force generated by the demand for political independence and the concomitant desire for economic progress.

By 1930, elected members had been introduced into the councils of Trinidad, the Windward Islands and Dominica. In no case, however, was there a majority of non-officials and in all cases elected members were in a minority. Jamaica had not received the proposed increase in elected members and although she enjoyed an official majority in the Legislative Council, had to be content with an elected minority. Meanwhile, British Guiana had lost her Dutch Legislative Institutions and with them the elected majority which had existed in the Combined Court. In 1935, British Honduras, and in 1936, the Leeward Islands, adopted elected minorities. These new vestments, however, were but the trappings of representative government. The franchise was restricted to a mere fraction of the population. As late as 1938, the registered electorate of Trinidad was 6.6 per cent of the colony's population, and the corresponding figure for Barbados in the same year was 3.3 per cent. Moreover, a wide gap yawned between the electorate qualification and that for membership of the Legislative Council was six times as high as the income qualification for registration as a voter; in Barbados the multiple was four.

The call for political reform grew louder and more insistent throughout the thirties. The economic depression brought to maturity the growing working-class movement and the demand for economic justice dominated the social scene. The initiative in political agitation passed to these working-peoples' hands and the need for social reform reinforced the demand for constitutional advance. Between 1935 and 1938, labour unrest produced a succession of serious strikes throughout the islands and attention was forcibly called to the need for remedial measures. As a result, in 1938, the West India Royal Commission was appointed with wide terms of reference "to investigate social and economic conditions in Barbados, British Guiana, British Honduras, Jamaica, the Leeward Islands, Trinidad and Tobago, and the Windward Islands, and matters connected therewith, and to make recommendations."

These movements of the thirties were, of course, centred in the respective colonies, and the traditional insistence on reforms in the individual legislatures was by no means dropped. Extension of the franchise and of the elected membership of the Legislative Council was the immediate demand. In fact, however, the situation had altered rapidly since 1921 when MajorWood (later Lord Halifax) had reported "the absence of popular demand of local opinion for federation." By 1938, the concept of federation had been transplanted and was flourishing in Westindian soil. The explanation of this lies almost wholly in the political situations which had developed during the period.

Neither the 1921 Wood Report nor that of the Closer Union Commission of 1932 had resulted in any substantial satisfaction of the demands for constitutional reform; as a result, Westindian leaders of the new labour movements struggled in an atmosphere of political frustration. Already, however, the practical advantages of cooperation had been recognised, and the system of inter-colonial conferences had established a basis of functional association. Gradually the idea began to take root that the path to political progress lay through a federal union. As a political entity, it was argued, the colonies, through a coordination of their economic and political strengths, would be in a position to establish their economic stability and demand their political independence. Economic prosperity and political freedom would be the twin products of federation. In any event, dominion status for a federal union held safer promise of attainment than self-government for the individual colonies. The idea possessed obvious attractions and it is noticeable that throughout these years whenever the need for social and political reform was advanced the claims of federalism were never far behind.

The West Indian Conference of 1932 was the first demonstration of the new movement. In that year the Closer Union Commission had been appointed, and when it was revealed that its terms of reference did not embrace either the possibility of a Westindian federation or the problem of internal constitutional reform, a number of grass-roots Westindian politicians gathered at Roseau in Dominica with the avowed purpose of elaborating proposals for federation. The conference was attended by representatives from Barbados, Trinidad, Grenada, St Vincent, St Lucia and the Leeward Islands. They decided that it was "desirable in the general interests" of those colonies that a federation should be effected, and they proceeded to design a federal constitution for the Westindies.

Let the flowing oratory of 'Captain' Cipriani of Trinidad, as he brought the Dominica Conference to a close, catch the fervour of those early Westindians:

"And now as I pull the curtain down on the final stages of this important and far-reaching meeting, and watch the West Indies take on her mantle of nationhood and dip behind the horizon like some threatening storm-cloud only to rise again on the dawn of a new day, I look forward and see in letters of fire emblazoned: 'The West Indies Must Be West Indian.' And through the dark and grim grey dawn methinks I hear a whisper saying 'West Indians awake - awake West Indians: Victory, Freedom and Liberty is yours."

The West Indian National League was formed at Roseau to carry on the work of the conference, but as an organisation it never played a real part in later developments. Nevertheless, political leaders in all the colonies kept the hopes of the conference alive and maintained a certain identity of purpose. As the Royal Commission of 1938 reported - "it is evident that throughout the British West Indies contact is being maintained between those in each colony who are most interested in securing rapid political progress, and constitutional developments, such as the widening of the franchise, in any area may be found to reinforce the strength of the movement for federation of the whole group."

Contact had indeed been maintained and the war years drew the Westindian colonies much closer together. United in a common cause, they achieved a new identity of purpose and of action which went a long way towards destroying the psychological barriers which in 1921 Major Wood had found so obstructive to "federating an archipelago." These developments gave added vitality to the federal movement. The ramparts of separatism and prejudice had been breached; contact produced understanding; association revealed how unfounded were many fears. A Westindian consciousness had developed to the point where Westindian nationalism had been born. On the other side, the inadequacies of ad hoc expedients born of necessity had been painfully demonstrated, and a recognition of the need for federation now replaced in many minds a vague appreciation of the advantages of cooperation.

But if the experience of the war years reinforced one aspect of the case for federation, it weakened it in another. Political frustration had enhanced the attractions of federation. Now, for the first time since the 1860s, the Westindian colonies really began to advance politically. 'Representative' government, which was the goal of the twenties, was now firmly established. 'Responsible' government which, even in the thirties must have appeared largely unattainable, was by the fifties within the grasp of Barbados, Jamaica, Trinidad and British Guiana. In all but Trinidad, reform of the legislature was virtually complete; universal adult suffrage prevailed in all the colonies.

Such reforms were, in the main, the product of the war years and those which immediately followed. They were long overdue and, having come at last, everything changed. Federation, in particular, which possesses an appeal as a possible alternative to improbable local self-government, began to be suspect for that very reason. Much emphasis, therefore, was laid in the post-war period on the need for a guarantee that federation would not in any way prejudice political advance in the individual colonies. It was a sentiment evident in many of the speeches at the Montego Bay Conference in 1947. The destiny of the Westindies was now moving into Westindian hands.

Montego Bay itself was preceded by a meeting of the Caribbean Labour Congress, which was really a meeting of leading Westindian political parties (other than Bustamante's JLP which was in office in Jamaica), asserting, as it were, their right to be heard, and heard in support, at the very outset of the federal process. The names of those present tell their own story: Grantley Adams, V C Bird, Robert Bradshaw, Hurbert Critchlow, Albert Gomes, T A Marryshow, and Norman Manley himself among many others 'knitting together,' as Rex Nettleford put it, 'the ideas of federation, nationhood and self-government.' Manley who led the Jamaica delegation put the matter thus:

"I put first, and I put above all other things, the desire to see in the future a West Indian nation standing shoulder to shoulder with all other nations of the world. Is that a large ambition? I say it is the smallest ambition that responsible people can utter in the face of history. I say that we in the West Indies can prove one great thing to the world - and that is that a people, none of whom are native to these territories, all of whom have for one reason or another been torn from their countries and brought here, partly willingly, partly by compulsion or by distress in their own homelands, that we with our many strands, from Africa, from India, from China, from an assorted variety of European territories - we are capable of welding the power of the diversity into a united nation.

"I pray, before God, if we can prove that to the world, we would have accomplished something which would write West Indian history large across the pages of history for all times. It is a problem to stir and inspire every man who knows anything about the long and bloody history of the common humanity beset and perplexed and torn by artificial divisions without any real meaning in the face of the purpose of life."

But, he added:

"...if we federate, we must federate as self-governing units who voluntarily surrender some of the power which each has over his own to the common whole. I reject totally any sort of mismarriage between colonial rule and federation, and I would predict for such a marriage such an abortion as politics has never seen; and I say that a federated

52

West Indies cannot aim at any smaller immediate objective than dominion status. I cannot imagine why we should be federating about if it is not to achieve the beginning of nationhood."

Alexander Bustamante was later at the Montego Bay Conference to assert with characteristic bluntness:

"Before I shall even advise the people of this country that they should have federation, I want to be told - and not just by word - I want documents to the effect that the same day federation comes the same day self-government comes."

The Secretary of State was quick to reassure the Montego Bay Conference on this latter point but, even so, the conference insisted on placing its position on record in terms of a resolution which recorded the view:

"that an increasing measure of responsibility should be extended to the several units of the British Caribbean territories whose political development must be pursued as an aim in itself without prejudice and in no way subordinate to progress towards federation."

The truth is that a race had begun which no one could have foreseen even ten years earlier between independence on an island basis and Westindian nationhood fulfilled through an independent West Indian Federation. It was a race 'federation' was to lose. For the time being, however, even at Montego Bay, there were few who imagined that independence was achievable at the level of the individual islands. Norman Manley could state the federal aspirations in terms wholly compatible with Jamaica's political goals. He did so in words characteristically elegant and penetrating:

"How to marry expectation with reality, how to create a larger field for ambition, how to overcome the disadvantages of being too small to be heard in a world where silence means stagnation, how to make a real culture and a real unity out of all the richness of our diversity, how to show the world that differences of origin and colour can come together on a level of tolerance and oneness, how to overcome distance and poverty; these are the challenges that federation faces and may meet to make a worthy end."

Norman Manley might so easily have become the father of the Westindian nation. As it was, when the moment to lead the nation came, political realities at home constrained this great man to stay at home, to decline the mantle of regional leadership and, ultimately, to take Jamaica to a separate independence.

This year, the Westindies might have been celebrating the 30th anniversary of the federation. I wonder what would have happened had Jamaica's referendum gone the other way? What would have happened had the decision taken at the 1961 Lancaster House Conference which settled outstanding details of the federal system and fixed the date for the independence of the federation, not been frustrated by the 'no' vote in the referendum? Perhaps the forces working for fragmentation - which led to both the referendum in Jamaica and the arithmetic of 'one from ten leaving nothing' - would ultimately have destroyed the federation, even in a post-independence context. We cannot discount it altogether but, somehow, I doubt that they would have succeeded had the vote in Jamaica been 'yes' and the Westindies became independent as a Federal Nation on 31 May 1962. I believe with John Mordecai that the tenuous Lancaster House patchwork would have held, that the federation would have grown stronger and faith in it firmer; that ultimately, Manley's early vision of a strong Westindian nation would have been fulfilled. Prospects for the Caribbean would now be very different.

But the present comes out of the past and, not surprisingly for the Westindies, it seems to come out of a rejection of federalism. Yet, in a sense, federalism never had a real chance to be tried. The truly West Indian Federal Constitution agreed in 1961 never ever became operational. It was not so much that federalism was rejected as that it lost out to separatism in the race to independence. In the result, however, the present has had to be built upon that reality with remembrance of the federal option, at most, as a yearning for what is not. The present has had to be constructed instead on a fragile regionalism. Having let federalism slip from our grasp, regionalism became a necessity, and we have spent the last 26 years - not always in total conviction - trying to make a virtue of it. That effort has been on the whole a triumph of practicality over inclination - the compulsions of mutual interest in regional co-operation overcoming our natural archipelago instinct for contrariness and fragmentation.

So, is the dream really shattered - the one I shared with Norman Manley 35 years ago at the LSE? Was the vision of a Westindian nation only a mirage? If we failed in the 20th Century, can we afford not to try harder as we approach the 21st? My answer, unequivocally is 'No' - the dream is not shattered; Westindian nationhood is not a mirage; we do have to try harder. There is something now almost evolutionary about Westindian unity: a historical rhythm reaching to fulfilment, a rhythm reinforced by the compulsions of present realities and future prospects.

Those realities, I suggest, compel Westindian unity both in how we perceive the world of the 21st Century and in how we act to secure a place of dignity for the people of the Westindies within that world. Yesterday was 40 years since the arrival of the 'Empire Windrush' bringing Jamaicans who would help in the reconstruction of post-war Britain and of their own lives which British colonialism had moulded.

54

They and other Westindians who came here so long ago from different parts of our archipelago have no doubt whatever about their Westindian identity. They need no counselling about solidarity and common purpose as they contribute to the multi-racial society that Britain is, and strive to make it a more just and equitable place for them to dwell in. They cherish their island origins, but there is no room in Brixton or in Handsworth for the petty irrelevances of island rivalry.

So it is, as well, in the wider world and will be increasingly on the economic fronts. Westindian governments, for example who face up to Britain's entry into the EEC in the 70s will face even more perilous problems in the 90s as the European Community becomes a single market with implications for sugar, for bananas, for rum, and for much else vital to the Caribbean's future. In that decade and beyond, survival is going to dictate real, not minimal, Westindian unity. We surely defile the memory of every slave and every indentured worker who laboured on Westindian plantations in the service of Europe if in our island postures today we become mimic men and women of a plantocracy that kept the Westindies apart so that they might better sustain their petty structures of economic and political power. We do well to reflect on this as we celebrate this year 150 years of the end of slavery in the Westindies and the beginnings of indentured labour. For Westindians that common heritage of bondage is a heritage of oneness also - within our countries and between them.

In the early 17th Century, as the first people of the Westindies were being displaced by the new arrivals from Europe and the 300 year regime of insularity was about to begin, John Donne was writing in England:

"No man is an Island entire of itself: every man is apiece of the continent, a part of the main."

Today, as we look to the 21st Century, the truth every part of the Westindies must respect and to which each Westindian must respond is that "No Island Is An Island Entire of Itself". Every inch of our Westindian region from Belize to Guyana is a piece of one nation, a part of one people, a bit of one world. The vision of Westindian Nationhood that Norman Manley cherished has only sharpened with the passing years. Its pursuit will remain our central challenge until eventually we reach it.

The Fourth Norman Memorial Manley Lecture

Given by The Rt Hon Michael Manley, former Prime Minister of Jamaica at the London School of Economics on 30 October, 1992

"Caribbean Cooperation - The Imperative for Survival"

igh Commissioner, Excellencies, Ladies and Gentlemen. That is the sort of introduction which for its generosity and because of its kindness, I think, reduces the subsequent agenda to an anti-climax but, nonetheless, I thank you most deeply.

I have to begin with two things in my mind, one involves an apology, not quite a *mea culpa* about the two cancelled lectures because I really did not arrange the illness that caused the first, nor the local crisis that occasioned the second, but I do apologise if it inconvenienced anyone.

As to the intimidation, let me put that right out on the table because if I do not get to relax I will never deliver this so-called lecture. I am intimidated first because it was in this building that I learnt forever the limitations imposed by God upon my intelligence. But I must tell you that one of the things I remember vividly, is the tremendous intellectual excitement of one of the great figures of this institution and indeed of history, and that was Professor Harold Laski.

I do not know whether this is the room, but it looks vaguely familiar, in which I used to sit with hundreds of others students, literally spellbound as Laski gave his lectures. He was not only intellectually fascinating but he had also a marvellous thing, that when lectured he lectured in paragraphs not sentences; I beg you to note the difference, and there was a point at which we all learnt that the big excitement as he developed one of these things where the paragraph was the sentence was, we would begin to wonder whether he would ever extricate himself from the convolutions, and he always did and he taught me this thing, (really not taught me, because I didn't learn it but I used to sit and admire it) about the power of superb intellect.

One other reason for being intimidated: well, I am surrounded by officialdom, I am introduced by a High Commissioner. I am in the presence of High Commissioners, but, worse than that, I am in the presence of a former Chief Justice of Barbados and, as I saw him, my mind began to race through, you know, now have I really done anything in a Caribbean context? (but I do thank you all very much for...) I even have my banker here which really has me terrified!

The occasion is, as the High Commissioner said, taking place at a very interesting and critical moment in Caribbean history. I have not had a chance today, because I think the five hour difference makes that impossible, to hear what came out of a vital Heads of Government Conference in Port-of-Spain on Wednesday, Thursday and today. That it was a very important meeting is self-evident. It was a meeting that was really called to consider some problems in the elaboration of our common market and our attempt at economic cooperation in the Caribbean, but, more importantly, to look at the recommendations of a body that had worked very hard for two years - The West Indian Commission - to consider the question 'Where now for the West indies?' - and I have only to say, that is to remind you, that it was headed by one of our great men of the Caribbean, Sir Shridath Ramphal, to give you some sense of the fact that would guarantee that it was relevant and important. And in getting ready for this and, forgive me, I do not write speeches any longer; when I write a speech it bores me and it is almost guaranteed that it will bore everybody else. You may not be spared the boredom but you may have a better chance if I do not write it and read it. But you know I went back to my late father, which is of course the over-riding cause of my sense of intimidation, and that was Norman Manley himself, and I went back to something that he said in his speech in Kingston in 1947 at a meeting of a body called the Caribbean Labour Congress, which the Trinidad High Commissioner and myself later helped introduce to the student body of the West Indies in London. And this is what he said in 1947:

"I say it is not hard to see what we are to do. The history of all nations is a history of amalgamations from small things to large. I say it is evident that we must create out of ourselves a large enough unit to

57

do two things. First to satisfy the growing ambition of our people for an area of action large enough for their creative energies: and the West Indies is full of creative energy, as full as any place in the world today. I say we must create a large enough area, small though it may be in the face of the colossal who bestride the world today, but a large enough area to give us a voice and pull and power over those international affairs which, in the long run, determine the peace and prosperity and the opportunity for happiness of the three million people of these lands.

"I say our second ambition must be to take what we have together to plan for a national future for our people. Let any man examine his conscience and speak for his own country and ask himself 'Do I feel capable?' And if we dare speak the truth, and this is an occasion when truth should be spoken, we are bound to admit that the very fact of size and the very fact of limitations imposed by that size makes the task almost insuperable".

One week later, Sir William Alexander Bustamante joined him in Montego Bay for an official Caribbean Conference and spoke with passion of the need to federate. Those things happened in 1947 and what is today's context? For the last two decades, the 70s and 80s, the world has seen a series of developments in which larger groups have been created by the voluntary act of sovereign states. The most dramatic and controversial at the moment is the European Community. There is the North American Free Trade Association of which Bush is partly the architect and which Clinton has said is correct although he has one or two caveats about how it might be developed. Our own CariCom, The East African Economic Community, the Andean Group and Latin American Free Trade Association, the Central American Common Market and, in all of those cases, we see what we call the process of aggregation by voluntary act. And then suddenly in the last two years we have seen a contrary phenomenon. The phenomenon of disaggregation in which first, the Soviet Union has literally fallen apart, disintegrated. Yugoslavia, Somalia ripping itself to pieces and so on and so forth, so that, as we look at the Caribbean today, and indeed as we look at the world today, at a superficial glance, we think we see one process that has been elaborating itself for the last 20 years and then, suddenly, a counter process. And it is beginning to look recently, and when you look, think of the problems of Maastricht, and John Smith announcing another way and Paddy Ashdown holding firm to unity. When we look at all of that, we might be tempted to feel that the forces that divide are overcoming the processes that unite.

Now tonight, I would like to look at four things:-
I would like to look more closely at what lies behind the forces that

are leading to unity as against those that are leading to apparent disunity. I would like, secondly, to consider what they may imply for the Caribbean.

Thirdly, to ask the question within you "Is N W Manley's vision as he expressed it in 1947 relevant today?"

And, finally, do the recommendations of the West Indian Commission indicate a path that we should follow?

Let me go back to what is really the natural historical point of departure for the discussion in the Caribbean. The attempt at federation that failed. Manley and Bustamante in 1947 set out very clearly why we should do it - why we should pull together this federal unitary sovereign state. Why did it break up? That is the great question that people ask themselves. It seemed logical, all the leaders of the time supported it. Why did it break? It broke for a number of reasons I would like to suggest.

I suggest firstly it broke because there was not within the common Caribbean experience at that time a natural set of social forces that would make it withstand a deliberate attempt by any significant element in the political process to break it up. Let me put it this way: if all of the leadership of the Caribbean at that time had decided to hold true to a path that all collectively chose, it would have survived.

On the other hand, where political development seem to challenge this hugely critical, hard-to-define thing that we call sovereignty, if it is ever challenged, sovereignty and the surrender of it, will only survive if there are huge, powerful, cultural, social and economic forces that persuade the people to resist the attempt to break it up and to make some structure survive.

The minute federation was challenged by Bustamante - and I have no quarrel about that, that is history - the question then arose: "What would the natural forces of the time make more likely to happen." And as one who as a young person fought tremendously hard in the referendum of 1961 by my father's side and with people like the second lecturer, Vivian Blake and others who fought to persuade the Jamaican people to stay inside the federation, I have long since had to go back and ask the question over and over: How do you analyse the dynamics of what occurred that led the Jamaican people, overwhelmingly, to reject the federal idea? And if I might summarise it, if it is of interest to you, and I think it is of historical significance, the reason was really quite simple - fear is a huge force in politics. He who can manipulate fear has got a massive weapon in his hand. You watch what is happening in Europe right now. If somebody is to contend against fear there is only one thing that they can put against it and that is the common sense of self-evident self-interest. I am sorry to say this - in my earlier more idealistic incarnation I would have come to that view with great pain I now come to that view with resignation.

One side was arguing 'If you federate, all these little poor people from the small islands will come to Jamaica and take your job in the cane piece.' And everybody you know suffers from the delusion of grandeur. It is very difficult to get Jamaicans to remember that there are as many people outside of Jamaica as inside: very difficult to get them to remember that Brooklyn which we are trying hard to colonise at this moment, having dealt with Brixton already, the second wave is right there is Queens and Brooklyn. They really forget that Jamaica is not quite as big as Brooklyn. So all of us you know, cherish the illusion of a sort of 'continental destiny.' I believe it is true even of the St Lucian or the Grenadian and very properly so - and I know it is true of Jamaicans. So everybody began to get this feeling: "If we stay in this federation I am going to lose my job." Now what could we argue? we couldn't invoke any concrete image of loss. We could only argue the hope of a future. The future will be bigger, it will be grander, it will have more opportunity; we'll have a bigger voice in the United Nations and people. I remember, in the cane piece hear somebody say "Is wah dat"; but nowhere - and this is one thing that one has to reflect about - nowhere was there the sense that if you broke up federation there was something to lose. For example, all our economic ties were in a classic manner of the Third World/North-South. We traded with America, we traded with Canada, we traded with Britain. Nobody had a factory whose management, shareholders and workers derived their livelihood from the sale of goods to Trinidad or Barbados or Grenada, St Lucia. So how couldn't you say "look, watch how you break this thing up you know, because you talking 'bout them might come take your job but you might lose you job in the Trinidad, Eastern Caribbean Market." So it was theory and hope versus fear, and fear did not win, fear wiped us out because it would always do that without the countervailing force of self-interest.

So let us say it could not survive, it did not survive, and as far as I am concerned, I am quite philosophically accepting that it may never happen. Maybe we do not ever need to do that, maybe it was an idealistic attempt that did not rest upon a sufficient foundation of cultural, social and economic commonality, perhaps. But what did we have to do the minute we broke up the federation? We had immediately to start to re-construct an arena for co-operation and within one year of breaking up the federation the talks had to start; how else can these little islands find a way to create an economic canvas of cooperation and opportunity. So we went through the business of CARIFTA - the free trade area - CariCom, which I was privileged to be a part of in 1973, and so on and so forth, and began to try to find the means to develop an economic framework that would make sense, facilitate co-operation and all the rest of it. And it is that process of reconstructing the challenge to the collective intelligence of the Caribbean and its leadership.

Why is it important? Let us see if we can revisit, what I humbly suggest, the fundamental forces at work in the world. Why is the process of aggregation taking place? Is it not, as politicians might like in their conceit to imagine, the result just of political intelligence. Politicians do not create history if they are very smart they react intelligently to the real forces that create it. And those forces, I suggest, are economic and are really determined, in the long run, by technology. Technology has, as the High Commissioner said, created the global village but I beg you to realise the 'global village' is not some term of art or some convenient phrase of rhetoric. It is only a simple way of describing profound changes that have been taking place in the way that production, distribution and finance have been organised over the centuries.

I am not going to bore you by going back to the industrial revolution and everything that happened since then. I am sure half of you know better than I. What I know now is that we live in a world in which technology is slowly making marginal that which we used to regard as the process of purely national production. Until quite recently people would think economy ... that England produces this, that and the other; France produces this, that and the other; Jamaica produces this, that and the other. That world is disappearing so fast it is almost hard to keep pace with it. You buy a car today: if you think that car was made in a country, you are not living in a real world. The car probably had part of it manufactured in South Korea, the ownership is probably rooted in Japan somewhere, you may find 15-20 countries have contributed something to the finance or the making of parts of that car. What you finally get is an assemblage of dispersed international production. Why? Because communication makes it possible. All the other technological changes make it possible and because in the end what an economy does is search for the rationale of the most efficient production. The politician may try to hold it back for good and sufficient national cause - part of a political process - but you don't defeat it in the end because in the end what will win is what technology makes logical. So we are looking at a world that more and more has dispersed sources of finance production, marketing distribution and the rest.

I will give you an idea: by 1983 the US Transnational Corporations controlled 75 per cent of all US exports. They weren't in the hands of national companies, they were in the hands of transnational companies and one half of US imports were bank figures.

By 1985 the UN had a study that showed that between one-fifth - I beg you to listen to these figures, they are staggering in what they imply - between one-fifth and one-third of the imports and exports of developed market economies were intra-firm transfers. They were not America exporting or Britain importing, they were transnational companies moving these things up and down within their corporate boundaries. That is a change in the way the world economy operates. And I suggest that in today's world, the smart countries are the ones who have the political wisdom to understand this, and to realise that it poses certain things for the way we view the nation-state and economic activity and development. And those nations that are learning to understand that reality are doing what? .... they are aggregating. Can you imagine? It is not difficult to imagine the United States and Canada; good neighbours with tremendous cultural commonalities - even look at the way that Toronto Blue Jays now use American and Dominican Republic Players to win the World Series. If that is not globalisation, talk to me! The Canada/US thing is easy to see. Imagine the US now going to enter into a formal free-trade arrangement with Mexico. Think back over your history. Think back over all the quarrels about the Mexican whetbacks pouring over the boundaries to steal American jobs etc, and how in the face of superior economic logic in one flash that is dismissed. I tell you better - I always say it with trepidation in any part of Europe. But up to 1939, every time any European had a quarrel you can be sure a lot of people died. Forgive me, but they wrote history in a manner that always invested death with almost mystical glory and I give them enormous credit for that, for he who can represent his misdeeds as an extension of virtue is really quite remarkable! And it took me a long time before I could disengage from the mysticism of these wars. But 1000 years - think about it - nobody will ever count the millions who died because somebody did not agree with somebody about something to do with economics in European history. And now post-1945 what we see is a triumph of rationalism abolishing 1000 years of historical habit. And it's not for me to interfere with other people's process, but he who turns back European unity, is not so bright...I am leaving tomorrow morning (laughter). And, of course, there are always tremendous difficulties when you have to move into something that in many ways is revolutionary... is now... to share any kind of decision making, is a huge challenge.

In fact my father in that same speech said, and I quote:

"I reject entirely and I reject for Jamaica and hope all the delegates will reject it for his own territory, the approach that begins by asking 'what can I get out of it?' If he tries to get all for himself all will lose everything"... Norman Washington Manley 1947 - Profound.

Let's now look at this other trend. I heard a debate in the Jamaica Parliament - happily not for me to reply to now that I am happily ensconced in the ranks of the unemployed. I do not have to leap to man the barricades everytime there is an argument, but I watch with amusement and interest and I heard it argued: How could you be talking about the Caribbean Commission now working for unity when unity is a discredited idea falling apart in the Soviet Union, disintegrating in Yugoslavia? Disingenuous actually. I am not bright coincidentally, by what is the truth? The truth is this. We have to draw a distinction between, I suggest, the areas where a kind of unity involving the surrender of sovereignty has been imposed artificially and by force, from cases where you move spontaneously by rational choice to cooperation. It is a totally different phenomenon.

What is the Soviet Union? The Soviet Union and its aggregate did not begin with Stalin, it began with Ivan the Terrible. You can trace it through Peter the Great, through Catherine, through Nicholas. What you were watching was the aggressive Russian chauvinism eventually brought to an ultimate refinement by Stalin with the Red Army, that was imposing Russian hegemony on half a continent. If Stalin had been able to deliver such enormous contentment in terms of rising standards of living and expanding horizons of opportunity and all the rest of it, people might have eventually given up their old instincts to individuality as people and nations and cultures.

But what was Stalin's failure to deliver in terms of people's lives and what they experience? It was only a matter of time before ancient cultures and groups would rip apart the thing that had stolen their sovereignty from them under, in the end, the power of the Red Army. Perfectly logical and totally different phenomenon. Yugoslavia, why is Yugoslavia tearing itself apart? Because if you go back to Croats, Serbs, the Bosnian Muslims, there if no natural historical unity in that group. Tito, in a triumph of his own resistance against Hitler, his quite remarkable personal charisma, his enormous astuteness as a politician, pulled together modern Yugoslavia and the minute Tito went, what you're getting is a reversion to ancient historical conflicts. Not one defends them - they are tragic, they are awful, but to confuse those processes of disaggregation with the formation of the European Community as if one is now replacing the other, is a historical nonsense.

So what does it mean for us? Have we in the Caribbean got a situation where some army since the 1950s has forced us all together against our wills?

No! Are we a group of people the Trinidadians have some deep desire to conquer and take over Jamaica? No! Do we have in our background some enormous hostility in which I really want leap across the podium and seize the former Chief Justice by the throat? No! In

63

fact, I am extremely fond of him. I look at my friend Ulric who together helped form the West Indian Students Union.

I remember the time when we discovered our common cultural heritage, did we not, as students here? So we have no ancient enmities that make it so difficult for us to co-operate. So what are you creating the difficulty about? Let me begin again (the Press is here). I done argue for federation. Maybe it will never happen, maybe it is not even necessary but what is important is the process of integration and co-operation. We have huge natural advantages - we have a common language; we have a large and common history; we have similar culture. I am glad the Sparrow provides a diversity although I feel in the end that Marley may be the one that really squares this up, and heaven knows we have not done badly with the cricket.

Though I see things are breathing down our necks recently, but you know cricket, we do, the West Indies University, who do, and infact we get on very well really, and you only have to look at the Caribbean people in England or America to see how naturally we co-operate, how naturally we have a sense that we are a part of a people rather than a number of peoples.

What did the West Indian Commission propose? It proposed a context that we should aim to remain a community of sovereign states - very important - they did not try to suggest that we compromise this touch of sovereignty. They proposed that we should have a Caribbean Commission, that we should aim for a single market, a common currency, a CariCom Assembly and, very important, the systems of co-operation including external relations. That is more so and more formally than happens naturally. It is a sort of minimum agenda for the new chapter. Where do we go from here? And once again I feel that as we did in 1961, the Caribbean faces a choice. What do we do? Are we going to demonstrate a maturity and go forward on the path of integration sensibly, pragmatically and with whatever constraints we feel should be recognised? Or are we going to be short-sighted, opportunistic. There is always one thing that can be played upon and it's the last serious point I make to you. In the very process of the way the world economy is evolving, where the transnational corporation becomes more and more the seat of decision-making, there is a consequence but I think also a partial remedy. The consequence is that people begin to feel increasingly remote from influence, remote from the feeling that they can, through their Parliament, affect economic decisions and how those decisions affect them. Therefore there is a tendency in the modern world to be - and you see it happening in the political process everywhere - a sort of disorientation. People know there are huge changes taking place. They feel that a new environment, a new political culture is emerging with which they are not familiar. They are not sure that the old buttons to be pressed are going to produce the consequences in decision-making. And this is an inevitable consequence of the fact that, as the world economy globalises, the direct influence of the nation-state is less immediate. It is an historical inevitability but it poses great strains. Smart countries are saying one answer is to aggregate. A totality that will one day stretch from Moscow to London has a better chance, if it can develop coherent policies within it, to deal with a globalising multi-national-type economy, than Britain by itself or France by itself, etc.

But it also means that to the politician it's open field-day for manipulation. For all the politicians have to do is to play upon the feeling that everything that's taking place is making you feel more powerless, more this, more that, and by appealing to ancient experience and present fear they can manipulate immediate discontent. Already as the West Indian Commission talks of going further on the path of integration, the cacophony of propaganda has started in Jamaica.

I am almost sorry that I was not there to reply myself, perhaps it was just as well - but it was dealt with very effectively and very rationally and correctly. But what was the cacophony about? We began to hear a shout across the Parliament - "No federation by the back door." I mean this is really going to the depths. I won't compare it with the recent experience of an election taking place in another country, but it is really going to the depths because nobody anywhere suggested anything remotely resembling federation. It is all a very practical, sensible - "Where do we go next?" But already "No federation by the back door", that's meant to terrify, to play upon old fears, and that is the first argument.

The second argument was "We don't want a Caribbean Commission", and let me make it clear that the proposal for a Caribbean Commission isn't for a Commission. If we don't have a Commission it is no problem. The real problem is: How do economic groupings secure follow-up to economic decisions?

Right now, the European Economic Commission does a tremendous amount of work, some of which is controversial, perhaps, but what it does is a huge amount of work to follow-up decisions of national government to see that things actually happen as they are said to be intended to happen. And if anybody can find better ways to do this than a Commission, then be my guest. A third thing being contended is a single currency faster than people can accept its implications, and if you have to pull back from it or postpone it, so be it. Never go faster than you can. But what underlies it? If you begin to move towards Exchange Rate Mechanism and things of that kind, it is true that on the one hand you are giving up immediate fine-tuning control over some of your economy and its macro-economic environment and that is a very difficult thing to accept politically. And so, therefore, as we say in

65

Jamaica, "Nuff respect to those who oppose it."

On the other hand, you cannot really conceive of an effective long-term, single functioning economic unit that does not have some kind of single currency, so you should never give it up as a long-term aim if you are serious, even if you feel you are not ready for it today.

And I always think to myself that if you have a single currency... let me put it down plainly... one of the things a single currency forces you to do is to be sure you deal with your productivity, you don't want a common currency because then you want to use the Exchange Rate Mechanism to hedge your bet against your productivity weaknesses by comparison, and if those are realities that are beyond handling at the moment, cool. But do not fool yourself that you are holding on to some permanent sovereign virtue because you are not. You are probably concealing a national productive failure.

(At this stage I know I am going to get thrown out of the country) (laughter)

But, equally, I say without hesitation and I say it for the Caribbean, if you are going to go into that kind of advance economic macro-engineering, then I support... in fact I would be a part of a demand for a social charter that ensured that the masses, the people, the workers of all categories did not become the victims of the process of transition and change. That is my philosophy.

I come finally to the argument about the voice in the United Nations about which my father felt so deeply. I heard it argued in the Jamaican Parliament: "What? Are we going to give up 12 voices in the United Nations?" and my mind went back over the theories of critical mass and I thought to myself that when all 12 voices speak... I tried to remember when last I saw a headline on page 27 column nine at the bottom, one inch of what any of those voices said. So you know, the thought as was argued in the Jamaican Parliament that "12 voices give us more to say" I conceive, but it guarantees that less people listen, and so therefore I am a strong supporter of the view of an integrated, as proposed, sort of foreign-policy mechanism, so that when we speak we carry one message, even if it is delivered by many persons.

And so, finally, I end with my thanks to you for your patience, your many years of forbearance in my failure to appear previously, and by simply saying once again, I think our people have a choice. I think to the extent that our overseas populations are sensitive to these issues; you can influence that choice, you can be a voice. What are the choices? Fear against courage: propaganda against wisdom. I do not quarrel with history, but what I do know is that if we fail to act to give to ourselves the advantages of a greater collective strength and planning, reality and voice, the generations to come will not forgive the leaders of today.

The Fifth Norman Manley Memorial Lecture

Delivered by Mr Bill Morris, General Secretary, Transport & General Workers' Union on Thursday 16 December 1993, Transport House, London SW1

"Rich World, Poor World: Squaring the Circle"

I feel extremely honoured to have been asked to deliver the Norman Manley Memorial Lecture this evening. Norman Manley is a towering figure in the modern history, not only of Jamaica, but of the entire Caribbean.

As a socialist, Manley also had a broader internationalist vision. He profoundly believed that collective effort and involvement was absolutely necessary to turn personal values and beliefs into realities. He helped to draw up the constitution of the People's National Party which now has strong links with the National Workers' Union and the TUC. This link with trade unionism is an important recognition of the importance of collective effort and action.

Throughout history and across the world, two forces have always been present in the liberation struggle. Wherever there is oppression, wherever there is discrimination, wherever there is disadvantage and inequality - organised labour and the churches have always worked for freedom. And Manley is identified with both.

Manley's life and work was a demonstration of that link. His ideas, particularly his commitment to Caribbean unity and internationalism, have a resonance throughout the world. Not just a story from the past, but lessons for today.

Today, global politics is characterised by changes on a scale not seen since the end of the second world war. After years of the horrors and iniquity of apartheid, Nelson Mandela is poised to become the President of South Africa.

Throughout the former Soviet Union and Eastern Europe, the dominant model of communism has collapsed and nations are grappling with the problem of building democracy. Even in the Middle East hopes for peace remain, as the Israelis and Palestinians try for the first time to reach some sort of accord.

Yet, to a large degree, these positive developments are tempered by an ugly rise in nationalism and chauvinism. The European continent is rife with examples. Last Sunday's electoral success of the extreme nationalists in Russia is just the latest. A week or two before, we saw the Northern League and neo-fascists emerge as powerful forces in the Italian elections.

This year also saw the election of the first British National Party councillor. Racial violence is on the rise across Western Europe - from Mostar in the former Yugoslavia to the inner cities of Britain. And, in the 1990s, the term 'ethnic cleansing' has entered our vocabulary as easily as the term 'the final solution' did in the 1930s.

I wonder what Manley, who stood so firm for unity in the Westindies, would have made of this madness. I am sure that he would not have missed the irony that political nationalism has re-emerged side by side with economic integration and the rapid globalisation of the economy. And I am sure that he would have recognised the compelling logic for increased economic and political cooperation among developing countries, against the background of economic globalisation.

In Europe, we still tend to discuss economic questions in terms of European, or even national, economies - when in fact we are operating in a global economy. This attitude is born, in part, from the seeds sewn in the past, through ideological selfishness. We have passed up many opportunities to share in the development of the economies of Eastern Europe and the Pacific Rim. Indeed, more often we set out quite deliberately to destroy those economies, seeing them not as potential markets for the future but as enemies of our system.

The same short-sighted and selfish approach led us to ruthlessly exploit the resources of Third World countries - not paying proper wages, and not making any investment to nurture and develop these economies as potential markets.

That failure to understand the global dependency of our economies still prevails to a large degree. And we are paying a price. Each of the three major economic blocs - the USA, Japan and Europe - are experiencing significant economic difficulties. The length and depth of the recessions we are now experiencing suggest that this is more than a mere cyclical problem. Frankly, this is no economic blip. There is something wrong with the very structure of the global economy.

So far, the response has been, not a collective effort to address the structural questions, but a retreat into what I call economic regionalism.

In the past, the economies of the industrialised West grew and expanded on the back of colonialism and exploitation. The peoples of the Westindies are only too aware that it was the economics of slavery which laid the foundation of the trading and financial might of Britain in the 17th and 18th Centuries. The slave trading nations of Western Europe have never compensated for the economic and social devastation which slavery brought to the people of Africa and the Caribbean. I will return to this theme later.

It was an irony that the very 'free traders' who gained so much from slavery and colonialism were happy to turn to protectionism when these instruments failed.

Today's world market does not offer the same simple solutions. It is shameful that slavery is still to be found in the world today. But it clearly does not have the economic significance of the past. And, following the second world war, the system of colonialism too has receded in significance - due in large part to the effort of liberationists such as Manley. Manley's legacy means that crude colonialism has no place on the globe today. Indeed, a significant number of the new post-colonial nations, particularly in South East Asia, present considerable (though usually quite specific) economic and technological threats to the OECD nations.

And, despite the fantasies of the 1950s and 1960s, space exploration has discovered no new markets. I am sure that Dan Dare and Captain Kirk would be disappointed to find that the US and Soviet space programmes are now little more, in economic terms, than hugely expensive technology demonstrators.

So, what of the second policy option - that of protectionism. It is now accepted, across the world, that national protectionism is no longer an option. Even if ideology and market economics are set to one side, modern technologies in transport, communications and other areas have made it impossible for any one nation, no matter how rich or powerful, to stand apart from the world economy.

For the most part, these technologies, and the production and marketing systems which have grown up around them, are no longer the preserve of national governments. The real economic power lies not in the White House or Westminster, but with the huge sprawling multi-national companies which control the exploitation of national resources, the production of finished goods and the delivery of services. It would take just two motor companies and three oil companies, acting together, to destroy the US economy. A handful of electronics giants, working together, could do the same to the Japanese economy.

Even in the sphere of macro-economic policies, the real power lies with multi-national institutions such as the World Bank, the IMF and GATT.

But the response to these developments has not been an abandonment of protectionism. The current GATT negotiations have demonstrated just how robust the protectionist instinct remains. It is the internal protectionist pressures within the United States, Europe and Japan which led to the two year delay in negotiating the Uruguay round.

What we are seeing is a trend towards larger, regional trade blocs.

The European Community - or European Union as it is now known - is both the longest established and the most advanced of these blocs. The Maastrict Treaty has formalised the single European Market and has set Europe on the course of monetary, and perhaps even political, union. If the EU can stand the strain of expanding to include the EFTA countries, and in time perhaps the East Europeans and even Russia and others of the former Soviet states, it will represent a massive single market. Not, perhaps, a 'fortress Europe,' but a formidable force in future negotiations on international trade regulation.

The EU will now be mirrored by the North American Free Trade Association - NAFTA. A combination of USA, Canada and Mexico will create a single market larger than the EU, even in its present form. And, of course, the countries of the Caribbean and Central America are already only too aware of the difficulties which this presents them with.

A third formidable bloc is emerging among the nations of East Asia, the Pacific Rim and the Antipodes. Today, by any criteria of measurement, it is in the East that real growth is actually happening. The Japanese cash mountain, the growth patterns of countries like Malaysia, Indonesia and other Pacific Rim countries, and the 'people power' of China all represent a very real threat to the competitiveness of Europe and the Americas. And I am not talking about production of cheap, shabby goods cobbled together overnight - make it quick and sell it cheap. I am talking about serious and sustained investment in skills and capital - it is happening out there and it will present a real future challenge to the West, as well as to the developing world. If you want evidence of this, you only have to look at British civil aerospace industry whose future now depends on the outcome of negotiations between British Aerospace and the Government of Taiwan.

It is true to say that the formation and consolidation of these trading blocs is really a question of institutions catching up with the existing reality of a world economy which is developing on regional and global lines.

Even without NAFTA, US jobs are moving 'South of the Border, Down Mexico Way'. AT&T, America's biggest telecommunications company, has moved its operations across the border to Mexico. A simple investment in six weeks training in English means that Mexican operators can be employed at ten or 15 per cent of the wages of US operators.

As a European trade unionist, I am well aware of the massive challenge - even danger - which this presents to European jobs. We have our own potential NAFTA right on the edge of Europe in the form of North Africa. Morocco has applied for special EC status, and, of course, there are many other North African countries wanting the same status. But we needn't cross the Mediterranean Sea - Eastern Europe too provides a potential NAFTA.

For us, the challenge cannot be interpreted as one of stopping or slowing these developments. Even if it were desirable, that option is not open to us. Indeed, if it is beyond the power of even the most powerful nation states, it is certainly beyond the power of a trade union.

The countries of the developing world face a similar challenge. The GATT negotiations have demonstrated that the size and power of the larger trading blocs and trading nations mean that they can determine the rules of world trade. Yet scores of nations, and millions of people, are on the outside. The entire continent of Africa, the countries of South Asia, millions of South Americans, and, of course, the Caribbean islands, are excluded from the powerful blocs.

How can developing countries avoid being marginalised in this situation? How can they find the space to develop and grow in this environment? If Norman Manley were with us today, I believe that these are the questions which would be exercising his mind. He is remembered as a great liberationist. But his vision was not just that of liberation from colonialism. It was of advancement for the liberated in a world where the old colonial order was increasingly irrelevant. A world where new models and new alliances would present new challenges to Westindians, with a new agenda to command. A world where development - even survival - would depend on the response of Westindian leaders to those challenges.

These challenges drove Manley's efforts to build a united West Indian Federation in the late 1950s and early 1960s. As we know, those efforts did not bear fruit. But history has vindicated Manley's vision.

Thirty years after liberation the economies of the Caribbean countries remain weak and vulnerable. With almost no manufacturing base, the Westindian economy is heavily dependent on the export of a very small range of agricultural products - primarily bananas and sugar. The only other significant income generators are tourism - which now

71

account for nearly 30 per cent of the regions' GDP and aluminium ore. The price has been debt and dependency. The term 'banana republic', shorthand for economies so weak and dependent that foreign companies can change their governments, was coined in the region. St Lucia and Dominica are single crop economies producing for a single customer. The British company Geest buys and distributes all the bananas produced in those countries. Without the skills and resources necessary to diversify, the cycle of dependency is complete. The economic destiny of the banana producers is not planned and developed by Caribbean governments, it is negotiated by European Ministers in the EC single market negotiations. A fall in commodity prices, or an alteration in the terms of trade can send national economies into a tailspin.

In his book 'Up the Down Escalator', Michael Manley, Norman Manley's son, drew attention to the power of the multi-nationals over the Caribbean's aluminium resources. Every attempt to force the bauxite companies to accept some responsibility for the local economy was met with fierce resistance by the multi-national cartel. The result - for every step forward, the cartel forced two steps back.

And today, recession in north America and Europe has a major impact on the growing tourist trade.

These are not simply questions of national pride - there is a real impact on the everyday life of the Caribbean people. Unemployment is high - over 20 per cent in some Caribbean countries. The tax base is narrow. There is a high dependency on imports - despite being essentially a rural economy, bills for food imports are increasing. Debt is pervasive. Poverty is rife. Crime, drug abuse and violence are on the increase. Emigration poses a constant threat to the economic and cultural future of the region.

If Manley were with us today, he would see that the majority of Caribbean populations are no better off in 1993 than they were in 1970.

Today, the Caribbean countries face the new and daunting challenge of NAFTA from an enduring position of weakness. In their trading relations with the north Americans, the small, open and fragile economies of the Caribbean face the real threat of competitive disadvantage vis a vis Mexico. The preferential trading agreements which the region has enjoyed in the past - such as the Caribbean Basin Initiative - can only be devalued by NAFTA. No matter what short-term concessions can be negotiated with the US Congress, through Sam Gibbons' 'NAFTA Parity Bill' or whatever, this remains the compelling logic of NAFTA.

Perhaps the only practical response is that it is better to be on the inside than left on the outside. But if any individual Caribbean state can negotiate NAFTA membership, it can only do so from a position of profound weakness. The combined output of the 24 Caribbean Basin Initiative countries is less than one per cent of the combined NAFTA output.

So what are the Westindian states to do? In the past, Caribbean countries have relied heavily on import tariffs. I believe that tariffs have a role in protecting emerging industries and economies. Unfortunately, that is not a widely held view in the modern international economy. Specifically, institutions like the IMF and the World Bank, on whom the Caribbean are so dependent, will continue to put the region under pressure to reduce external tariffs. In any case, it is increasingly clear that, though they may have a role, tariffs can never isolate an economy from the realities of the international economy - particularly for countries which are dependent on trade in such a small number of products.

This is not to say that all the problems can be solved by adopting the prevailing economic ideology of the North. Unbridled liberalisation can only lead to further weakness. You can find examples in the Caribbean of countries which have gone down the path of rapid and extensive deregulation and privatisation. We are also witnessing this experiment in Eastern Europe and some of the former Soviet states. Speaking as one who has lived and worked in the country which pioneered this strategy - if I can call it that - I see little evidence that it can deliver the goods over time. What is certain is that it is a painful process which hits the poorest hardest. And it is an extremely destabilising process and a process which is likely to reinforce dependency rather than encourage economic independence.

There are no quick fixes - no magic solutions. But Manley was absolutely right when he identified Caribbean integration as a way forward. He would have been saddened to see that, despite the comprehensive region integration projects which have characterised the international economy in recent decades, the Caribbean is still only stumbling towards a collective economic identity.

His dream of a West Indian Federation collapsed in the early 1960s - that is history. Despite the formation of the Caribbean Community - CariCom - in 1973, there has been little tangible progress towards integration in three decades up to 1990. That was time wasted.

In 1989 the West India Commission - headed by Sir Shridath Ramphal who delivered the 1988 Norman Manley Memorial Lecture - breathed new life into the project. The title of the Commission's report 'Time for Action' could not have been more appropriate. Although it ruled out federation, it argued that as regional integration picked up pace around the world, the Westindies risked being left behind as 'mini-

73

states'. It reminds its readers of the old Westindian maxim, "the hand is stronger than the fingers", and argued for joint sovereignty over a range of operational economic matters.

I am pleased to say the many of the report's recommendations were adopted by CariCom in the 'Port of Spain' protocol of 1992. The CariCom states have agreed that they must take decisive steps towards closer integration. I believe that Ramphal's report puts the integration debate on a new and much more positive footing. The focus has shifted from that which divides and differentiates, to that which unites:

* The geography of the region;
* The common cultural heritage;
* The shared legacy of colonialism and slavery;
* The collective experience of liberation.

There needs to be an urgency in the integration project - for the world will not wait for the Westindies (or any other region) to catch up. The Caribbean needs to build on 'Time for Action' to develop policies for community development and for tackling poverty. Policies to promote investment and exports. And policies to alleviate the crushing burden of debt.

In this respect, the Caribbean shares common problems with the rest of the underdeveloped world. Even with integration, the region will still be highly dependent on trade. It will still be heavily influenced by world developments. I suggest that this simplifies a need to extend co-operation for jobs and growth - and there needs to be a wider project of 'South-to-South' co-operation among developing countries.

Some may be sceptical about such an ambitious agenda. I would point to the significant - albeit limited - success of political co-operation through the Non-Aligned Movement in the United Nations, during the years of the Cold War, as an example of what can be achieved.

Against the background of the debate on European integration, some of you might think it strange to hear a trade unionist advocating regional integration so strongly. Of course, I am speaking tonight not just as the leader of the Transport and General Workers' Union and a socialist, but also as a Caribbean!

My union's attitude towards world economic developments have been guided both by the principles of trade unionism and the principles of internationalism. Indeed, the latter is an intricate part of the former. Economic and political realities mean that we have had to engage in the debate about European integration. When the livelihoods of my members depend on these developments, I cannot afford to stand on the sidelines. But we have not simply accepted the terms of the debate. We have pursued our own agenda within Europe.

That is why we have argued that a single market is not enough.

74

Neither is monetary union or political union. We have argued for a co-ordinated European-wide policy which addresses unemployment, growth and inflation. In particular, we have said that the problem of sustained mass unemployment demands a solution because it threatens not just our economic security, but the social cohesion of our societies and, indeed, our continent. And we have said that improved rights and protection for workers, together with legislation which guarantees equality, must go hand in hand with market and economic integration. I am sure that the labour movement in the Caribbean will take a similar attitude.

Indeed, I would go even further and say that regional integration is not enough. Global economic problems require global solutions. That means that we cannot content ourselves with protecting Europe's competitive position in world trade or establishing a more stable economic base in the Caribbean. We must go further and address global problems of poverty, underdevelopment, displacement and the environment. Needless to say, this is rather more than the European government's have in mind at the moment!

But it is a basic principle of trade unionism - and a principle which, I believe, Manley would have shared. Trade unions were formed on the principle that an injury to one is an injury to all. And they exist out of the belief that the only way to improve things for individuals is through collective action. These beliefs do not evaporate once you cross a national frontier.

Yet it is true to say that there has been a tendency, throughout the history of trade unionism, to take a rather defensive position on issues of international trade. I believe that, in an increasingly internationalised economy, there is no place now for this tendency.

Economic and social inequalities, both within and between states, is an increasingly obvious feature of our world. The economies of the OECD countries are extremely well developed. Their technological advantage has reached optimum levels. Billions of pounds, dollars and yen are spent to make even the tiniest technological improvement to products or processes. Indeed, similar sums are spent on marketing products in the hope of winning a little more market share.

Once again, the minutiae of the GATT negotiations demonstrates that there is little competitive edge left at this level of the world economy. Improved growth is now only possible at the margins. The OECD nations are in an ever more desperate search for new markets, but the narrow attitudes of the past have ensured that those markets have simply not been developed.

Even if we put the ideal of internationalism to one side for a moment, enlightened self interest demands that we look again at this situation.

75

We do not need yet faster motor cars. We do not need ever more sophisticated weaponry. We do not need more and more gadgets to perform the simplest household tasks. It is time to look again at the glaring needs which do exist in the modern world. And it is time to think about turning these human needs into economic markets.

Even within the OECD countries, we see the development of the two-thirds, one-third society. Two-thirds who have, and one-third who do not have.

At the same time, economic growth has gone hand in hand with environmental degradation. It is almost 25 years since the first man landed on the moon. Yet today, it can take perhaps two hours to cross London in a car. There is a glaring need for investment in basic environmental improvements - in water, clean air and sewage systems. And there is a strong case for demanding that multi-national companies meet the environmental costs of their activities in developing countries. Perhaps this could be done through a 'percentage club' for inward investors, whereby they pay into a fund to clean up the environmental mess which they have left behind in so many countries. These issues need to be addressed if we are to live in a stable, secure and sustainable society.

At a global level, the list of unfulfilled human need is even more striking. We live in a world of hunger, disease, ignorance, pollution, homelessness and unemployment. For many, it is a world without hope.

It is time that we invested to address these needs in the developing world. And, of course, this would hold many advantages for the developed world as well. For there would be new markets, new technologies and new investment opportunities.

The modern Western European economy was built on the Marshall Plan. Following the second world war, the Americans poured billions of dollars into the European continent. It was a specific commitment to rebuild the economies of Western Europe to ensure political stability in the short-term, and economic stability in the long term. That investment relieved a lot of hardship. But the plan was not devised for entirely altruistic reasons. It was born of economic self interest.

It is time to consider something similar today, to address the dual problem of underdevelopment in the South and economic stagnation in the North. But any such project must be driven by more than mere self interest, and more than some sort of charitable concern for underdeveloped nations. West Europeans have a duty to compensate for the economic and social devastation which the slave trade caused. This year, there has been in Britain a re-emergence of claims for reparation payments from Japan for the suffering and deaths suffered by British prisoners of war. I believe that there is a much stronger case for reparation payments from Britain to the peoples of Africa and the Caribbean

76

to make up for the injustices of slavery. This is not merely a moral duty, or even a question of equity - it is simply a question of justice.

We could begin by reviewing the crippling debts which do nothing for economic development and serve only to drain money out of the real economy. We should also consider a strategy for development similar to the Marshall Plan - perhaps financed by a proportion of GDP from each of the OECD countries. These resources could then be used for real investment in the economies of developing countries. Investment in training and skills so that economic growth is both tangible and sustainable throughout the world. We need a 'General Agreement on Investment and Growth' to complement the GATT talks.

The economies of the developed world are in decline. In many senses, the complex web of trading blocs and trade agreements is doing little more than recycling the misery and recycling the unemployment. At macro-economic level, we have to consider a standstill in living standards in the northern hemisphere over a sustained period of time - perhaps ten or 20 years. I do not mean that we must accept the inequality and poverty which exists in the rich world. But that must be a question of redistribution of the wealth which already exists. I am talking about a period of time when we eschew further improvements in the speed of motors cars and speed boats and invest instead in the developing economies where new, and real, markets can be created. The result would be real economic and social development for all the people, and all the nations, of all the world.

A project of this scale would indeed be an ambitious project. But the Marshall Plan was ambitious too. I believe that any possible way out of the protectionist loop has to be considered. Any proposal for squaring the circle of underdevelopment in the South and stagnation in the North is worthy of serious debate. The essence of any such strategy must be, not exploitation, but interdependence and responsibility. It is entirely reconcilable with the trade union principles of internationalism and self help.

I think that Norman Manley would have approved of this global approach. His experience in the liberation struggle led him to understand that, in the modern world, independence was a means to freedom, not an end in itself. He believed that success could only come from recognising that nations are interdependent, and that they must work together for the common benefit of their peoples. The nations of the Caribbean have come to accept a great deal of Manley's vision. I hope that the wider world community will one day do the same. Only then can we guarantee that "the people shall govern."

Glossary

Caribbean Basin Initiative. A preferential trade agreement between the USA and 24 Caribbean and Latin American countries. It defines a range of tariff-free goods which are imported into the US duty-free. NAFTA will remove much of the advantage of the CBI because CBI countries will be unable to compete with Mexico once tariffs between Mexico and the USA are removed.

NAFTA Parity Bill. A Bill introduced into Congress by Sam Gibbons (sometimes called the 'Gibbons Bill). It would relieve some of the adverse affects of NAFTA on the CBI countries by giving them trading parity with Mexico in the export of certain products.

CariCom. The 'Caribbean Community' established in 1973. It has 13 members made up of the English speaking Caribbean countries plus Belize and Guyana. It has a total population of 5.5 million. Its current goal is to establish customs, union and a common market by 1994. In the past, CariCom has made slow progress towards the creation of a common market. CariCom also has trade and technical agreements with Venezuela, Mexico and Cuba, and is negotiating with Columbia.

Port of Spain Protocol. Signed at a CariCom meeting in 1992. CariCom members agreed to speed up the process of integration, setting the target of customs union and a common market by 1994. They considered the 'Time for Action' report, produced by the West India Commission which was established in 1989 under the leadership of Sir Shridath Ramphal. Many of the report's recommendations were adopted, including: a CariCom Council of Ministers; a CariCom Supreme Court; a CariCom assembly of parliamentarians; and a Charter for Civil Society. However, CariCom rejected the report's proposal for a CariCom Commission and measures to close loopholes which allow for tariffs of up to 35 per cent in some Caribbean trade.

Lome Convention. Signed in 1975, the Lome Convention governs trade between Europe and the ACP (African, Caribbean and Pacific) Group in a range of products including bananas. This was the subject of disagreement in the EC, as countries like Germany wanted to see equal access to the European market for so-called 'dollar bananas' (primarily from South American countries). There was a compromise in the EC which reduced the tariff on 'dollar bananas' to 20 per cent with reduced controls on the volume of imports.

NAFTA. The North American Free Trade Association. Trade agreement between Canada, the USA and Mexico.

The Sixth Norman Manley Memorial Lecture

Delivered by The Rt Hon Tony Benn MP at the Commonwealth Institute, London on Friday 7 July 1995

"A Vision of the Future"

Your Excellencies, Your Worships, Friends and Comrades, it is a very great honour indeed for me to be invited to speak. It is the 102nd birthday almost of Norman Washington Manley - the name Washington I presume was given to him because he was born on July the Fourth - but nobody can confirm that; and I am especially glad to be asked because if the editor of Wisden or Norman Tebitt had been asked to suggest a suitable Westindian speaker, I doubt whether he would have trusted somebody who came from England to put his heart into the job. I had the great honour of meeting Norman Manley and Michael, of course I know.

I succeeded in Bristol, when I was first elected in 1950, Stafford Cripps to whom reference has been made, and reading the previous lectures and hearing the High Commissioner, you are reminded, and I don't intend to go over it because you know it all - what an absolutely mythical character Norman Manley was - a great scholar, a lawyer, a distinguished parliamentarian, a soldier, a world statesman, founder of the People's National Party, an athlete, a teacher, a founder of the nation - someone who really contributed immensely to the development of Jamaica and to its place in the world.

And when I was thinking and discussing what I might say and what I might take as my subject, I thought instead of trying to go over that well-known ground, it would be perhaps most respectful to his memory to look at some of the issues that confronted him in his life, and project them into the next century: because he was born in 1893, you see which was the 19th Century. We are almost through the 20th Century and in no time at all we will be in the 21st. So I thought I would try and look, if you will bear with me, at some of the questions that he had to face and let me start with the question of imperialism.

Of course, the word imperialism when it was used in English in the 19th Century, was considered a very respectable thing because if you were an imperialist it meant that you were going to do well in British politics. It was assumed that Britain had a role in the world which was better than anybody else's. Queen Victoria, the Empress of India, not only ran a large British Empire including Jamaica but, when she died, two of her sons - rather, two of her grandsons - one became King of England and one became the Kaiser of Germany and her granddaughter married the Tsar of Russia. So the world was run by Queen Victoria's grandsons. And while the colonial peoples were being repressed by Queen Victoria's grandsons nobody thought much was wrong because that was the imperial idea.

It was the Russian Revolution in 1917 that produced the first anti-colonial super-power. Previously all the super powers, if that was the word to use were engaged in some way in a colonial control and now, with the collapse of the Soviet Union, I must say this in retrospect. Whatever you might think of Joe Stalin, and I must tell you under the Stalin regime I would be in the Lubianka or sent to Siberia very quickly for what I would have said about it, the existence of an anti-imperial, anti-imperialist super power had a profound influence on the National Liberation Movements because everyone who was engaged in every country, every nation, trying to engage itself in liberating itself from an imperial power was, in a sense, looking to Moscow to provide some support and that fact has to be remembered. But, of course, with the collapse of the Soviet Union, there really is only one super-power left and it is the United States of America.

And when George Bush pronounced at the end of the Gulf War a new world order, what I put to you for your consideration, and I do so very delicately, was that President Bush and now President Clinton have inherited the mantle of Queen Victoria. They run the world. They have armies all over the world. They have control of huge chunks of the world! They have client states whom they support and NATO (The North Atlantic Treaty Organisation) - which was set up in order to resist the possibility of a Russian attack on Western Europe, has now become an out-of-area force which can be used anywhere in pursuit of the interests of the European states now forming into a union and the United States of America.

So imperialism doesn't really die. It is always there, but it may be transferred from one nation to another. For example, Julius Caesar occupied Britain in 55BC. It was the first attempt to get us into the European Union, and he brought with him a single currency, pounds, shillings and pence, and we still spend it, and the Romans lasted from 55BC to 610AD. So there is nothing really new, and people who have given up their socialism on the grounds that they have a globalised economy had better look at their history, because they will find that history does tend to repeat itself.

So I think if we are looking at imperialism, the reason I mention this is there is this tendency to say: "Jamaica is free, the colonial powers are free, imperialism is over, we have won that! - Now isn't it marvellous!" It isn't quite like that at all.

Now the second point I want to touch on was the question of racism because there was inbuilt in the imperial idea, the idea of racial superiority. I think it was Rudyard Kipling who was the great poet of the imperial period, who talked about 'The White Man's Burden' that we had. Somehow God had chosen us to govern other people of a different race and it was a terribly heavy responsibility which we discharged with some regret but a great sense of duty. It was absolute nonsense! It was the oppression of some people by other people, and the myths associated with the old imperial idea do still persist.

Sir Paul Condon today has come out with the remarkable news that most muggings are done by Black people. Well, I've got news for him! All the corrupt policemen in Britain are White! Every single policeman who has ever been corrupt is White! And most young people engaged in crime are unemployed. They don't mention that because unemployment would raise a different question from racial prejudice.

So you must not think it's over. And then of course there is an element you know in racism to do with religion. The great religions of the world have tended to look down on other religions. For example, the struggle between Christianity and Islam goes back a very long time to the Crusades when we sent an army to conquer Saladin in the Old Palestine. Richard Coeur de Lion, whose statue stands up outside the House of Commons, was sent to fight Saladin who was actually a Kurd.

I went to Algeria a little while ago and met a former foreign minister of Egypt he said to me "We have had a seminar on the Crusades in Egypt," and I said "What did you discover." He said, "Well I discovered one thing, that during the Crusades, the European arms manufacturers supplied arms to Richard Coeur de Lion and to Saladin."

So nothing has changed and there is a terrible danger, you know, of investing your own national purposes with some religious importance that God is on your side, and of course if you have different gods, he will be on two sides and before you know where you are, it's your duty to God to kill people of another religion and what the Bishops in England call a Holy War is what the Islamic people call a Jihad. We talk about a

81

Just War, they talk about a 'Holy War,' and these things are deeply embedded in the public consciousness.

Then of course, you have to look at slavery, because slavery, the transhipment of millions of people from Africa to the New World was probably one of the greatest crimes that was committed in history. Torn from their villages, sent in ships, many of them dying on their way to the plantations in the New World. Somebody sent me the other day an article in the *Economist* about slavery. About 1840 I think it was, and the *Economist* said "Well you can't abolish slavery, you've got to regulate slavery." So you understand where those ideas of regulating the electricity and gas boards come from!

I represented Bristol for 33 years in Parliament, and Bristol made a lot of its money out of slavery. Some of the great benefactors in Bristol with statues up, were benefactors because they made their money out of slavery. And now there is a movement which I am very interested in, I am taking part in a television programme about it shortly, on the Africa Reparations Movement, that the African states are entitled to claim reparations for slavery, and although it may be rather a long shop legally, it is a very good case morally. If the question could be looked at not so much in those terms, but what about cancelling the Third World debts as a way of dealing with that, then we might make a bit of progress.

Then you have fascism and racism because you have a lot of unemployed people. In Germany in the1930s there were six million unemployed. Hitler found it convenient to blame the Jews and of course the Herren Force, the Master Race, the white blond nordic types who Hilter honoured, were kept in order by finding somebody else to blame, and it is true in this country as well. As unemployment rises, instead of saying it's a rotten economic system - I'll come to that later - people will say it's all those immigrants who came, and that's a very dangerous thing.

Now I come to another issue. I mentioned imperialism and racism (I am doing an examination course now). "What about nationalism?" The term nationalism is widely denounced. "Oh, he is a nationalist they say." But, you know, all the anti-colonial movements were nationalist. In the sense that they wanted freedom for their countries, and I think you've got to be very, very clear when you talk about nationalism in distinguishing between xenophobic nationalism where you hate peoples of another country and nationalism as a demand for democratic self-government of your own country. The desire for democracy was what inspired Norman Manley when he campaigned for universal adult suffrage in Jamaica, which was not won until 1944. So much for British respect for democracy.

It was only 51-years-ago that Jamaica got Universal Franchise but nationalist movements were in fact a very important element; and the Indian National Congress and the African National Congress were all about getting control for the people as a whole. I remember meeting Mr Gandhi in 1931 when he came to London. I was only six and I don't remember what he said except that he took a lot of interest in the little six-year-old boy, and you know what parents are like - they pat you on your head and talk to your parents. But he listened and a journalist said to him on his visit "What do you think of civilisation in Britain, Mr Gandhi", and Gandhi said, "I think it would be a very good idea."

So, you see now if you look at the question of democracy, then you come up against the question of federalism; and it's very important because Norman Manley was disappointed when the West Indies Federation was rejected, and I wouldn't dream of commenting upon that, but we are now engaged in Britain in a very interesting argument about whether we should or should not become part of a fully European Union. Indeed the recent discussion in another political party has touched on this in the last week or two.

I think it is very important that if you look at the question, because I was born a European and I will die a European, to recognise that the form of government that there is, is very, very relevant to your future, and my objection to a European Union, I tell you candidly, is that I do not see why we should be governed by bankers in Frankfurt and commissioners in Brussels we did not elect and can't get rid of. Now, that's nothing to do with not liking the French or Germans - actually Germans suffered more under Hitler than we did. But what sort of Europe? How is it to be governed? I think that whole question is a very important one, because you can have federal structures where the federalism is used as an excuse simply for taking control from elected people and putting it in the hands of others. So be very careful before you denounce - not that you would, I feel sure - legitimate democratic national movements.

Now I would like to turn to another subject, not mentioned very often, called capitalism.

The Labour Party, as you know, does not discuss socialism anymore and I don't want to embarrass them, but you would be surprised we do not discuss capitalism because it is the system we live under. If you look at capitalism, and I come to its power today because it's a very old idea, but not the oldest idea of all; because if you look at very primitive societies in Europe and everywhere else, you'll find common ownership was very, very common and then gradually, the privatisation of the land. In Britain, the earliest example of privatisation, the Parliament representing the rich stole the common land and handed it to rich farmers

83

and feudalism grew.

Private ownership became dominant and capitalism meant ultimately that industry was privately owned. And then you had the power of finance, to begin with, very slow in its impact but always there, and this question now has to be asked. "How do you deal with what is called 'a globalised capitalist economy.'" Don't muddle up globalisation with internationalism, they are totally different things. A globalised economy is one where the power world-wide is exercised by those with money. Internationalism is one where we find common ground with our own fellow human beings in other parts of the world in trying to improve our common lot.

And the more I think about this whole question of modern international capitalism the more relevant it seems to be not only for the point of view of countries like Jamaica, but of course for Britain and every other country as well. I give you one reason. There is, as you know, very, very tight control of immigration into Britain. Capital can move where it likes but labour can't move. Supposing that you have shares in the Chesterfield Manufacturing Company and it is not doing very well. So you ring up your stock broker and say, "I would like you to sell my shares in the Chesterfield Manufacturing Company. Would you please transfer them to Sony in Japan where I understand they are opening a new factory which is likely to be very profitable?" You can do that just on a computer and a telephone.

But if I live in Chesterfield and I work in Chesterfield Manufacturing Company and they close the plant, I can't go to the Labour Exchange and say "By the way, I hear there is a new Sony factory opening in Japan. I'd like to go there and my mum in the old peoples' home, and my son who is slightly disabled and granny - Oh we'd all like to go and get a job," because labour is controlled and capital is free. And that is the absolute hypocrisy really of saying we believe in a global economy. If it was a global economy everyone could go anywhere in search of work, but Western capitalism does not allow that, because as you'd know better than most, very, very tight control is exercised over the movement of labour.

And the more I think about this so-called market economics, the more I think it is a political and not really an economic strategy. Unemployment is deliberate. I tell you what unemployment does. It's very simple. It frightens people into doing what they are told. That's what it's all about. You get four million unemployed, and then, you may have a job. You go to your employers and say, "I can't live on the money." They say, "Oh, there are four million people who would love to live on the money I'm offering." And so it depresses wages, weakens the trade unions, boosts profits and provides control.

Similarly, it may seem a funny thing to say, but I think homelessness is deliberate; because if you have a job and you walk along the Strand and you see somebody in a carboard box, the thought comes into your mind, "if I have a row with my employer and I can't keep up my mortgage and I am dispossessed, I'd be in a cardboard box, so I'd better not have a row with my employer." And the more I think about this, unemployment is the discipline and of course fear is the way in which it's done.

But since we are talking about a globalised economy, and I know Bill Morris touched on this last year, let me just give you some of the figures that I came across in preparing this lecture, about the brilliant success of world capitalism. First of all, according to the World Health Organisation, one-fifth of the world's 5.6 billion population are living in extreme poverty. If you look at Oxfam, the richest fifth of the world's population lives in the industrially advanced countries and have average incomes 30 times higher than the poorest fifth.

Poverty related diseases claim the lives of 35,000 children every day.

Half a million women die in the world every year from causes related to pregnancy and inadequate health care.

Approximately 1.3 billion people have no clean water or sanitation and as the recent conference in Copenhagen revealed, one billion people in the world live on less than one dollar a day.

Now, whatever you may say about it, and how you tackle it, nobody is going to tell me that capitalism is a wild success from the point of view of the human race. And billions of pounds are spent on weapons and we were told for years, "the Red Army was about to come to London." I found it hard to believe that the Red Army would take over West Germany, Italy, France, come here, deal with Ken Livingstone, go to Northern Ireland and cope with Ian Paisley. What was it all about? After all they did not do well in Chechyna from a military point of view. How would they hope to manage here? But the point is, they want to stop socialist ideas spreading and it was really convenient to say there was a Red Army threat. Then if you are making the sort of speeches I am making tonight, which are very moderate as you will notice, you could say, "That man is an agent of the KGB. He is somebody working for Russia."

So that's what the whole thing was really all about and as you can see, even in Russia now, cholera has broken out, diphtheria has broken out, Zeltsin, they never tell you he was secretary of the Moscow Communist Party, because he is engaged now in the agent of bringing capitalism into Russia. The Mafia have taken over and don't think what interested the West in Russia was democracy. I tell you, I know that, for when they opened the first MacDonald hamburger joint in Moscow, Mrs Thatcher said it was the sign that democracy had arrived.

85

Well I had never linked that with at all. I am only thinking aloud about those things that would have concerned Norman Manley in his time, and will concern future generations. What's really happening? I tell you what what's really happening. The BBC economic correspondent of the World Service wrote an article in the *Financial Times* the other day, and this is what he said:

"Some countries, especially in Africa, if they were to be run along the lines of commercial enterprises rather than states, investors find them more attractive." He was saying - this is the BBC after all, the voice of BBC - telling the world he didn't think governments are wanted anymore. He wants it run by companies, and then he puts at the end very openly, "What room does this leave for democracy?" The question can be asked everywhere, he said.

In a world where the bond markets dominate much of the decision-making process of the wealthiest nations, democracy is in one sense on the way out. Don't make any mistake, the use of market force is the end of democracy. I mean they are doing it already, with contracting out services. It won't be long before they don't have by-elections. If there is a vacancy people will put in a bid. Say, if I died at Chesterfield, it could be that Lord Jeffrey Archer would put in a bid for £100m and someone in the Labour Party may put in a bid for £50 and on polling day the returning officer would say "I declare ... the winner." Well I'm not kidding you at all. Indeed if they put the Prime Minister's job out to tender, I'd do it twice as well at half his salary. So, I am trying to say and I am trying to make it entertaining, but what I am really saying is that what Norman Manley fought for, which was the ballot box, would give you some control over your destiny but is now being taken away again in the guise of competitive productivity and so on.

And we've got a new religion. It's always been a religion and it's coming back 'Money!' Do you ever listen to the news? - The business news at night? The Dow Jones Industrial Average. I don't know who Mr Dow Jones is but by God he works hard, you've got to give him that. Falls up and down every night - I hear the pound sterling has dropped three points decimal against a basket of European currency - I have never had a basket of European currency - sounds a handy thing to take on holiday! But as soon as the pound sterling drops, Virginia Bottomely closes three hospitals and the pound sterling rises because you've got to satisfy the gamblers. Take Mr Leeson in Singapore. Where did he get £800m to lose on the Tokyo Derivative? I would like to know the answer to that. Now in case you think this is all dangerous left wing propaganda, I bought *News Week* the other day, 'Does Government Matter? said *News Week*. The state is withering and global business is taking charge - *American Magazine*. As government

86

influence wanes, what binds the world together is increasingly multi-national business.

So what I am really saying, and I am not trying to diminish in any way Norman Manley's achievements, but if you think he won freedom for the people of Jamaica you may be absolutely wrong. He won political freedom from Britain but the power of business is taking over Britain and Jamaica and everywhere else and that is a question we actually have to address.

I often wonder how they do it. It is not in the interest of anybody this should happen. What language do they use? One of many things it took me a long time to realise, you must have realised it a long time ago, is the word "customers". Get on the train now and the ticket collector says "customers who boarded the train at Derby will look after their baggage". So when he came round, I said 'By the way, just a word," - a very polite word (he is a member of our RMT union) I said, "I am not a customer, I am a passenger." He looked at the book by Rail Track and he said, "I am very sorry, you are a customer now." So I said, "If I go to hospital for an operation, am I a customer or a patient?" Well, Rail Track didn't advise him on that particular question. I said, "If I am hauled up for driving, drunken driving, does the magistrate say 'customer at the bar?' Does the Archbishop of Canterbury talk about 'our beloved customers'?"

But the thing about a customer is this, if you haven't any money you can't be a customer. So they find a word that dehumanises, depersonalises the poor, so you never have to think of them again. And after all, if you ask me to pick the people who need houses most in the whole country, it's the homeless, but they are not customers - they haven't got the money, so they don't exist. And that is modern capitalism, and I haven't said a word about Conservative ministers because I don't think it's got much to do with them. I did mention Virginia Bottomley.

I think we have got to be very careful we don't allow this philosophy to grip us and capture us because it is a very, very powerful religion. The reason is it suits all the rich and powerful people that it should be our religion.

Now, of course, against that you do look and see what the alternatives are. Trade unionism was an attempt, and Norman Manley was involved in that with his cousin Bustamante, in trying to build up trade unions, because trade unions discovered that the only way you could beat capitalism is by banding yourself together, and that is the basis of trade unionism, collective action. So people came along and analysed it a bit more carefully.

Karl Marx, that old Jew worked at the British Museum long before Stalin came to power. You can't blame him for what happened in Russia any more than you can blame Jesus for the Inquisition.

Marx was working only in the British Library and he came to an interesting and obvious piece of information that there was a marginal difference in interest, economic interest, between those who slogged their guts out creating the wealth and those who earned it and that was what Marx contributed. It wasn't actually Marx who did it alone because Adam Smith, the economist Mrs Thatcher most admired, said: "The rich are the pensioners of the poor." The rich live on the backs of the poor and that has always been the case.

So then, you say, well out of all these ideas, where did trade unionism come from. Well it didn't come from Joe Stalin, you know. I was brought up on the Bible and I remember the Book of Genesis. I don't know how many people nowadays are brought up on the Bible, but those of you who weren't let me tell you: There were two brothers called Cain and Abel; and Cain killed Abel and the Lord had a word with him about it and said: "But why did you do it?" And Cain said: "Am I my brother's keeper?" Now that question, 'Am I my brother's or my sister's keeper?', is the basic socialist question, because if you are your brother's keeper, then an injury to one is an injury to all. United we stand, divided we fall.

"You do not cross a picket line" did not come from the Kremlin. It came from the Book of Genesis. Trade unionism is the human response to the brutalities and injustice, and I think for that reason that it is very important that a trade union should have a political voice as well. Which is why I am a member of the Labour Party, and if I were asked from the top of my head, which I haven't been asked, to think of an objective for the Labour Party in the next century, I might say something like this, correct me if I am wrong: "Perhaps we are there to secure for the workers by hand and by brain the full fruits of their industry and the most equitable distribution thereof as may be possible on the basis of the common ownership of the means of production, distribution and exchange." So you see what I mean. These ideas are still alive and you can't eliminate them just because you change things at the top. I don't think that apartheid ended in South Africa because Nelson Mandela amended Clause 4 of the African National Congress Constitution.

So now let me turn to the question of socialism, because Norman Manley was a socialist, and as the High Commissioner said, a lot of the ideas in Jamaica came from trade union or socialist tradition of the party of which I am a member, and socialism is a very old idea. See, people speak as if it was a foreign import from Leningrad in 1917, but my assessment, and tell me if I am wrong, is that in every country in the world, in every period in history, there are always two flames burning in everybody's breast, the flame of anger against injustice and the flame of hope in which you can build a better world, and that is what socialism is about. And the idea, the reason it's linked to common ownership, is because it was always about democratic control of economic power.

The High Commissioner referred to Manley's last speech in which he said it is economic independence that we want. People want democratic control and in the Acts of the Apostles, forgive me if I am quoting the Bible twice, I sound like Billy Graham, but I am increasingly beginning to feel like Billy Graham, all things were in common. In 1381, the first time they tried the Poll Tax on us, there was a Vicar called Rev. John Bull who said things would not get well in England until all things are held in common. In the English Revolution when we got rid of King Charles (we had a little trouble then, I won't go into it, it could happen again and I probably should not refer to it either) but in the English Revolution, the Levellers said: "The earth is a common treasury. It is a crime to buy and sell the earth for private gain."

Now if that had been at the Rio Summit on the Environment, we might have made a little progress: communism failed because it wasn't democratic, but I think that in the next century we should see the recovery of socialism. Because I have an idea, I may be wrong and I am an optimist, that the end of communism is going to be of significance to socialism as the reformation was to Christianity.

They took on the Vatican who got above itself and what it did was to liberate a newer and more popular form of Christianity, and I think the same could happen as a result of the collapse of the communist states; and that's why I think that, when we look ahead, the rational planning of the world's resources will soon seem to be the most obvious and commonsensical solution that you could find, and if you abandon any concept, any internationalistic idea of justice which is what socialism is about, then you get all these.

Now, can I turn to one other thing that Norman Manley was very much involved in, because he was a great parliamentarian and he was immensely committed to the parliamentary system. I have been there 45 years now for my sins and I look at Parliament and I assess what's really happening. First of all we are very boastful about Parliament. We have had it now for over 700 years , but women only got the vote at the same age as men in 1928. So democracy, which is quite different from parliamentarianism, is quite a new thing.

Jamaica only got the vote, as the High Commissioner said, in 1944 when I was already an adult in the armed forces, and our democracy is very limited anyway. I mean, you don't have a hereditary president in Jamaica; we are still stuck with the Queen in the House of Lords and all you are allowed to do is elect the House of Commons. You can't get into the House of Commons without swearing an Oath of Allegiance to the Queen. Before you get there you have to say: "I swear by Almighty God that I will bear faithful and true allegiance to HM Queen Elizabeth, Her Heirs and Successors according to Law." Dennis Skinner read the Oath and said, "When she pays her income tax" - and a few weeks later she did. If you don't do that you can't sit. Dennis felt it was worth making the extra addition.

But you see, we have got into the situation and I am being deadly serious where democracy has become a spectator sport. You sit at home and it's what happens when Jeremy Paxman interviews John Redwood and you are not expected to do anything about it. You watch Peter Snow and whatever his name is with the computer who tell you who is going to win the next elections, who is going to win the Olympics, who is going to win the World Cup but you, you've got nothing to do with it at all. You just keep out please, it's our turn now.

I was in College Green - you've probably seen it on the television where all those journalists meet - and it was an extraordinary sight. I went with my video camera because I am making a film about what happens in Parliament (you will have some surprises when its shown by the BBC at the end of the year) but there were these princes of the media standing there with their lights and microphones and make-up girls interviewing a handful of Members of Parliament and the public were just watching, absolutely watching. There is no politics discussed on the media anymore; it's only personalities, and all about who is doing this, who's doing that, who is going up, who is being disloyal. Nobody ever asks me this when I go to my constituency. Nobody ever asks me whether Virginia Bottomely would be reshuffled, whether John Major would survive.

They say to me "Tony, they've closed the pits, I haven't a job, my son can't get a grant to go to college, my daughter is married, can't get a house, my auntie can't get a hip operation, grand-dad can't live on the pension. That's what it's about, but they don't discuss that on the BBC. The media is the new church. It tells you what you've got to think because it says so on *News Night*. And I tell you, we've got to be very careful we don't allow the parliamentary system - in which I believe I would not work there - to be taken away from us.

Now I finish with just one or two points. I hope I have stayed within the remit of 'A Vision of The Future.' To look at this last century in perspective, really what happened in the 20th Century is a huge development of technical power. At the beginning of the century the fastest vehicle travelled at 60 mph. Now spacecraft can go at 25,000 mph. At the beginning of the century the most people you could address was by shouting through a megaphone now you can address the population of the world on a satellite. At the beginning of the century

90

the largest number of calculus you could make was on your fingers and abacus, now you can do millions and millions in a micro-send on a computer. In the beginning of the century the largest number of people you could kill was using a Lewis machine gun; now you can kill millions with the A-bomb, and the escalation of power makes the democratic question the most important.

I am a great believer that democracy and openness are the best remedies for the abuse of power. I have developed five little democratic questions which I offer you. If you have heard them before forgive me, but if you meet a powerful person, it might be Joe Stalin, it might be Adolf Hitler, Jacques Delor, it might be Robert Maxwell, it might be the head of IBM, you ask them five questions:

1. What powers have you got?
2. Where do you get them from?
3. In whose interest do you exercise them?
4. To whom are you accountable? and,
5. How can we get rid of you?

Now that's the democratic question, because if you can't rid of the people who govern you they will never bother to listen to you. I am up at 5 o'clock in the morning to Chesterfield. Everybody I see in Chesterfield is my employer - the street sweeper, the bus driver, the ticket collector, the home help - they employ me and could sack me so I have to listen to them.

If you talk to the commissioners in Brussels or the bankers in Frankfurt or the people on Wall Street they don't have to listen because you can do absolutely nothing about it. And so, if I sum it all up, I think that if you look into the future with the inspiration of Norman Manley's life and work, and what a fantastic achievement in his life to have brought Jamaica to Independence to a new role for itself in the world, but if you look at our job it is going to be very difficult indeed and if we don't root our politics on morality - what I meant is that you should always argue is it right or wrong, and not whether is it profitable or loss making.

You can argue about what is right and wrong and have some interesting arguments about it, but don't let profit be put automatically, unquestionably above the interests of people, democracy and internationalism. And remember something else, and I will finish with it, that if you want a change it does not depend on charismatic leaders, and I know Norman Manley was charismatic. Certainly when I met him I was bewitched by his personality; when I see that lovely bust there, I am reminded of the strong and principled man. But political change is not brought about simply by leaders, but by people. It is when people do something that something happens.

91

There is an old Chinese philosopher I often quote because I strongly agree: Lou Soo, I think was born some 2000 BC. This is what Lou Soo said about leadership and I think it applies brilliantly to Norman Manley. Lou Soo said: "As for the best leaders, the people do not notice their existence, the next best, people honour and praise, the next best the people hate, the next best the people fear, but when the best leader's work is done people say: 'We did it ourselves'."

I believe Norman Manley inspired a nation to so believe it had done it itself, and that is why it is worth commemorating his memory and continuing with the lectures so that none of us forget the quality of the leadership that he gave to his people and to the human race.

Thank you very much.

Biographical Notes

Professor Stuart Hall

Born in Jamaica 1932. Educated at Jamaica College. Rhodes Scholarship in 1951 to Merton College, Oxford, where he read English. Jamaica Scholarship for post-graduate research at Oxford in 1954. Founder-Editor of *New Left Review*. Research Fellow, then Director of the Centre for Contemporary Cultural Studies, University of Birmingham, 1964-79. Currently, Professor of Sociology, the Open University. Married with two children.

Lord Caradon

Baron (Life Peer) cr 1964; Hugh Mackintosh Foot, PC 1968; GCMG 1957 (KCMG 1951; CMG 1946); KCVO 1953; OBE 1939; b 8 Oct, 1907; son of late Rt Hon. Isaac Foot, PC; *m* 1936, Florence Sylvia Tod (*d* 1985); three *s* one *d. Educ*; Leighton Park Sch., Reading: St John's Coll, Cambridge. Pres. Cambridge Union, 1929; Administrative Officer, Palestine Govt, 1929-37; attached to the Colonial Office, 1938-39; Asst British Resident Trans-Jordan, 1939-42; British Mil. Administration, Cyrenaica, 1943; Colonial Secretary: Cyprus, 1943-45, Jamaica, 1945-47; Chief Sec., Nigeria, 1947-51. Acting Governor: Cyprus, 1944, Jamaica, Aug. 1945-Jan. 1946, Nigeria, 1949 and 1950. Capt.-Gen. and Gov-in-Chief of Jamaica, 1951-57; Governor and Comdr-in-Chief, Cyprus, Dec. 1957-60; Ambassador and Adviser in the UK Mission to the UN and UK representative on Trusteeship Council, 1961-62, resigned; Minister of State for Foreign and Commonwealth Affairs and Perm. UK Rep. at the UN, 1964-70. Consultant, Special Fund of the United Nations, 1963-64. Mem., UN Expert Group on South Africa, 1964; Consultant to UN Develt Programme, 1971-75. Visiting Fellow: Princeton, Havard and Georgetown Univs, 1979. KStJ 1952. Hon. Fellow, St John's Coll., Cambridge, 1960. *Publication:* A Start in Freedom, 1964.

Hon Vivian Blake, OJ

Born March 1921, Cambridge, St James, Jamaica. Educated Cambridge Primary School 1926-31, Wolmers Boys School, Kingston, Jamaica, 1932-39. Employed Jamaica Civil Service 1939-45. Called to the Bar the Hon. Society of Gray's Inn, London, January 1948. Admitted to the Jamaica Bar March 1948. Appointed Queens Counsel, Jamaica, April 1958. Private practice in Jamaica and the Caribbean, March 1948 to July 1973. Past President of the Jamaica Bar Association and Jamaica Bar Council. Member of the Executive

Committee of the Peoples National Party, Jamaica, 1952-69, for several of those years a Vice President of the Party . Member of the pre-Independence Legislative Council, and then the Senate, 1961-67. Leader of Opposition business in the Senate, 1964-67. MP for the constituency of South-East St. Elizabeth, 1967-72. Appointed Minister of State, July 1973, Member of Parliament for the constituency of North-East St. Ann, September 1973-July 1978. Minister of Industry and Commerce, 1973-78. Appointed Judge of the Supreme Court of The Bahamas, September 1978, and subsequently became Chief Justice. Retired September 1983. Now practises in Leicester, England, as Legal Consultant to overseas clients.

Sir Shridath S Ramphal

Sir Shridath (Sonny) Ramphal is Co-Chairman, with Swedish Prime Minister Ingvar Carlsson, of the Commission on Global Governance, whose report *Our Global Neighbourhood* put forward proposals for far-reaching international reforms.

He was Secretary-General of the Commonwealth from 1975 to 1990, after having been Minister of Foreign Affairs and of Justice of Guyana.

Sir Shridath served on each of the five independent international commissions which reported on global issues in the 1980s: The Brandt Commission on International Development, the Palme Commission on Disarmament and Security Issues, the Brundtland Commission on Environment and Development, the Commission on Humatarian Issues and the South Commission.

He was Chairman of the West India Commission, and is a member of the Carnegie Commission on Preventing Deadly Conflict. Currently he is Chairman of the International Steering Committee of LEAD International - the Leadership for Environment and Development programme, of the Board of International IDEA - the International Institute for Democracy and Electoral Assistance in Stockholm, and of the Advisory Committee of the Future Generations Alliance Foundation in Osaka.

A member of the Council of the International Negotiating Network set up by former US President Jimmy Carter and the Board of Governors of the International Development Research Centre of Canada, Sir Shridath is also Chancellor of the University of Warwick and the University of the West Indies.

He was President of the World Conservation Union -IUCN 1990-93, and was a Special Adviser to the Secretary-General of the UN Conference on Environment and Development - the Earth Summit, in Rio de Janeiro in 1992. His book, *Our Country, the Planet,* written for the Earth Summit, was printed in several languages.

As Guyana's Foreign Minister, he was twice elected Vice-President of the United Nations General Assembly. He served as Chairman of the UN Committee for Development Planning 1984-87.

A lawyer, Sir Shridath studied at King's College, London, Gray's Inn and the Harvard Law School.

Rt Hon Michael Manley, OM

The Right Honourable Michael Norman Manley, Former Prime Minister of Jamaica, has had many careers as journalist, trade union negotiator, politician, international statesman, author, and scholar. Born in Kingston, Jamaica, in 1924, he is the second son of the late Rt. Excellent, Norman Washington Manley (Premier of Jamaica, 1955-62, and National Hero of Jamaica) and Edna, nee Swithenbank (sculptor of international repute, and one of the founders of Jamaica's modern art movement). He was educated at Jamaica College (1935-1943), and was an Honours student at the London School of Economics where he read for the Bachelor of Science degree in Economics (1945-49).

From 1949-1952, Mr. Manley worked as a journalist, with the BBC (London) and later as Associate Editor of *Public Opinion*, a Jamaican newspaper. From 1952-1972, he was trade union negotiator, serving as President of the National Workers Union of Jamaica, and founder and first President of the Caribbean Mine Workers Federation. After being elected as President of the People's National Party in 1969, he became Jamaica's fourth Prime Minister after a landslide victory by the Peoples' National Party in 1972; was re-elected by an even greater majority in 1976; his party was defeated in the 1980 general elections.

During his years in opposition, before being re-elected in 1989, Mr. Manley undertook a major re-examination of Jamaica's economic strategy and became one of the first social democratic leaders to accept the need for a strong market economy as the best framework for dynamic economic growth, while continuing to develop pilot programmes aimed at significant social transformation. [After winning a third landslide victory in 1989, Manley retired from political life in 1992.]

Michael Manley has been a strong advocate of the need for Caribbean regional integration, having been a major architect of CariCom (Caribbean Community). Since his retirement, he has been the catalyst and interlocutor with all the major leaders in the Central American and Caribbean region formulating the programme for the creation of the Association of Caribbean States. He is also Chairman of the Caribbean Development Tourism Task Force. He was actively involved in helping to engineer the involvement of the United Nations in assisting the restoration of democracy in Haiti.

Mr Bill Morris

Born Bombay, Jamaica; educated: Mizpah School, Manchester, Jamaica and Handsworth Technical College. Positions held within the Transport & General Workers' Union (T&GWU) Shop Steward - Hardy & Spicers, Birmingham (1963); Northampton District Secretary (T&GWU) (1976); National Secretary for Passengers Services Trade Group (1979); Deputy General Secretary (1986, 1981/91). Other positions of responsibility held: member of General Advisory Board - BBC and Independent Broadcasting Authority; Chairman of the Labour

Party's Conference Arrangements Committee; member of the EC Economic and Social Affairs Committee; member of the Commission for Racial Equality (CRE) and member of the Prince of Wales Youth Business Trust. Currently as T&GWU's General Secretary, he chairs the Trade Union Congress' (TUC) Task Group on Representative at Work; the TUC Youth Committee and the TUC Regional Councils Consultative Commitee. He is also a member of the International Transport Workers' Federation's Executive Board; a representative for the Union on the Council of the Advisory, Arbitration and Conciliation Service; a sitting member of the Employment Appeal Tribunal and a member of the governing body of two universities, Nene Northampton and Luton. Bill Morris holds honorary degrees from Southbank University, Leeds Metropolitan University and the Open University.

Rt Hon Tony Benn MP

Born 3 April 1925. He served in the RAFVR from 1943-45, learning to fly in Africa and commissioned as a pilot officer.

He served briefly in Egypt, and was then transferred to the Fleet Air Arm as Sub Lieutenant RNVR 1945, training at the Royal Naval College, Greenwich.

He was first elected to the House of Commons in 1950. He has sat as the Labour Member of Parliament for Chesterfield since March 1984, and for Bristol South East from 1950 to 1983. He was elected to the National Executive Committee of the Labour Party in 1959 and was Chairman of the Party in 1971-72. He has been a Cabinet Minister in every Labour Government since 1964 holding the positions of Postmaster General, Minister of Technology, Minister of Power, Secretary of State for Energy, and one-time President of the Council of Energy, Minister of the European Community. He contested the leadership of the Labour Party in 1976 and 1988.

He is the author of over 15 books.